ASH'S JOURNEY

Published in Great Britain 2024 by Farshore
An imprint of HarperCollins*Publishers*
1 London Bridge Street, London SE1 9GF
www.farshore.co.uk

HarperCollins*Publishers*
Macken House, 39/40 Mayor Street Upper,
Dublin 1, D01 C9W8, Ireland

Written by Gemma Wilkinson-Lowe

ISBN 978 0 00 861672 4
Printed in Bosnia and Herzegovina
001

A CIP catalogue record for this book is available from the British Library.

Stay safe online. Farshore is not responsible for content hosted by third parties.

This book contains FSC™ certified paper and other controlled
sources to ensure responsible forest management.

For more information visit: www.harpercollins.co.uk/green

ASH'S JOURNEY

A VISUAL GUIDE TO ASH'S EPIC STORY

CONTENTS

Ash's Journey to Become World Champion.......6
Who is Ash Ketchum?.............................8
Ash's Pikachu.....................................10
How Ash and Pikachu Met.........................11
Pallet Town.......................................12
Professor Oak.....................................13

THE KANTO REGION

Welcome to the Kanto Region 14
Badges Ash Won 15
Ash's Catches 16
Misty...18
Brock...19
Team Rocket 20
Trainer Tips......................................22
Trainer Tales 24
Battle Breakdown 28
The Indigo League Conference 32

ORANGE ISLANDS

Orange Islands 36
Badges Ash Won 37
Ash's Catches 38
What's Team Rocket Up To? 39
Professor Ivy 40
Tracey Sketchit 41
Trainer Tips......................................42
Trainer Tales 44
Battle Breakdown 46
Orange League Finals 48

THE JOHTO REGION

Welcome to the Johto Region 52
Badges Ash won 53
Competitions......................................54

Ash's Catches 55
Professor Elm 56
Casey...57
What's Team Rocket Up To? 58
Trainer Tips......................................60
Trainer Tales 62
Battle Breakdown 66
The Whirl Cup 70
Johto Silver League 72

THE HOENN REGION

Welcome to the Hoenn region 76
Badges Ash Won 77
Ash's Catches 78
Professor Birch 79
May 80
Max 81
Team Magma 82
Team Aqua...83
Trainer Tips......................................84
Trainer Tales 86
Battle Breakdown 90
Hoenn League Championship 94
Battle Frontier 98

THE SINNOH REGION

Welcome to the Sinnoh Region 100
Badges Ash Won 101
Ash's Catches 102
Professor Rowan 104
Dawn 105
Team Galactic 106
What's Team Rocket Up To? 107
Trainer Tips......................................108
Trainer Tales 110

Ash, Paul and Chimchar....................112

Battle Breakdown 116

Lily of the Valley Conference...........120

THE UNOVA REGION

Welcome to the Unova Region 124

Badges Ash Won 125

Ash's Catches 126

Professor Juniper 128

Iris and Cilan 129

What's Team Rocket up to? 130

Team Plasma....................................131

Trainer Tips......................................132

Trainer Tales 134

Battle Breakdown 138

Vertress Conference 142

THE KALOS REGION

Welcome to the Kalos Region...........146

Badges Ash Won 147

Ash's Catches 148

Professor Sycamore..........................149

Clemont..150

Bonnie and Serena 151

Trainer Tips: Ash and Greninja 152

Trainer Tales 156

Battle Breakdown 158

Lumiose Conference 162

THE ALOLA REGION

Welcome to the Alola Region............166

Z-Crystals 167

Ash's Catches 168

Z-Moves...169

Pokémon School...............................170

Professor Samson Oak......................171

Professor Kukui 172

Ash's Alolan Classmates 173

Alolan Island Trials 174

Ultra Guardians 178

Ultra Guardian Missions 180

Trainer Tales 182

Manalo Conference 184

THE GALAR REGION

Welcome to the Galar Region 188

World Coronation Series 189

Ash's Catches 190

Dynamax and Gigantamax 191

Professor Magnolia 192

Goh 193

Chairman Rose 194

What's Team Rocket Up To? 195

Trainer Tips......................................196

Trainer Tales 198

World Coronation Series 200

Return to the Kanto Region 204

Chloe..205

Cerise Laboratory Research 206

Project Mew 207

Trainer Tales 208

World Coronation Series 214

Travelling With Old Friends 220

Let's Go Home!.................................222

What is a Pokémon Master? 223

ASH'S JOURNEY TO BECOME POKÉMON WORLD CHAMPION

ORANGE ISLANDS

Ash headed to the Orange Islands on a mission for Professor Oak and to gain his four league badges. Ash defeated Supreme Gym Leader Drake to become Champion of the Orange League!

THE HOENN REGION

Next up on Ash's journey was the Hoenn region, and the Trainer prepared to take on the championship. Unfortunately, Pikachu met its match in Tyson's Meowth.

THE KANTO REGION

In his home town in the Kanto region, Ash partnered with Pikachu and began his journey to become a Pokémon Master! Ash lost to Ritchie in the Indigo League Conference.

THE JOHTO REGION

Ash was ready to gain eight badges in the Johto region needed to participate in the tournament. He battled valiantly against Harrison but was ultimately defeated in the Johto Silver League.

THE SINNOH REGION

The Sinnoh region provided many new challenges for Ash, and he gained a lot of skills. They weren't enough to take down his opponent in the Lily of the Valley Conference.

THE KALOS REGION

Ash faced Alain in the finals of the Lumiose Conference in the Kalos region. They appeared to be evenly matched, but Ash-Greninja was knocked out by Mega Charizard.

THE GALAR REGION

It had all led to this. The Galar region was home to the World Coronation Series tournament, the Master Eight. After a gruelling number of battles against many worthy opponents, Ash won the championship with his loyal Pikachu. He was crowned Monarch and could officially call himself a Pokémon Master!

THE UNOVA REGION

The Trainer made it to the quarter-finals of the Vertress Conference in the Unova region, but Lucario was too powerful against Pikachu.

THE ALOLA REGION

The Alola region was where Ash learned Z-Moves, which took his battling skills to a whole new level. The Trainer was strong enough to defeat the Masked Royal and win the league.

WHO IS ...
ASH KETCHUM?

From the moment he received his Pokémon licence when he was ten years old, Ash knew he wanted to be the best Pokémon Trainer there ever was!

Ash is brave, kind, enthusiastic, determined and confident, and he has a love of adventure. Although his confidence can sometimes bubble over into arrogance, Ash has a huge heart. Sometimes he can be too stubborn, but eventually he is able to admit when he's wrong. He wants to do what's best for his Pokémon and his friends.

Throughout his journey, Ash has been able to learn from his mistakes, and use his gym battle losses to get better as a Trainer. He never lets a defeat hold him back, and tries to instil this resilience in his Pokémon too.

Ash is extremely loyal and hates to break promises to his friends, family and his Pokémon. He is also willing to help people and Pokémon he doesn't know. He is always ready to make a new friend!

Ash is passionate about working hard to attain his ultimate Trainer goal, but he happily gives his time to help others achieve their dreams if he can.

SKILLS

- Climbing: Ash was once described as a 'human Mankey' for his amazing climbing skills.

- Aura: This ability allows Ash to sense a Pokémon's feelings. After obtaining the Key Stone, Ash's Aura powers increased.

- Bond Phenomenon: Ash can use this special transformation with his Greninja, increasing its strength. This can only be achieved when there is trust between the Trainer and their Pokémon.

- Z-Moves: Ash obtained a Z-Ring allowing his Pokémon to perform these powerful moves. He even has an exclusive Z-Move with Pikachu known as the 10,000,000 Volt Thunderbolt.

- Gigantamax: This changes the shape or size of the Pokémon. Unlike some Trainers, Ash is able to Gigantamax his Pikachu without it having to return to its Poké Ball.

- Mega Evolution: Ash does this with his Lucario making it ultra powerful in battle!

- Empathy: Ash is great at considering Pokémon's feelings. He knows the Red Gyarados needs his help at Lake Rage.

ASH'S LOOK

Ash's look has evolved over the years, including his iconic baseball cap. From the origin of the fingerless gloves in the Kanto region, to the stripy tee in the Alola region, Ash definitely has a unique sense of style!

KANTO / JOHTO REGION

HOENN REGION

SINNOH REGION

UNOVA REGION

KALOS REGION

ALOLA REGION

GALAR REGION

BATTLE STRATEGY

In battle, Ash is great at problem-solving and thinking on his feet. He finds a way to win by using the special and unique abilities of his chosen Pokémon and championing their differences. His relationships with his Pokémon is what leads to his success on the battlefield!

ASH'S PIKACHU

Ash's Pikachu is a very special Pokémon – we guess that's why Team Rocket are always trying to steal it! Pikachu's abilities, both in and out of battle, are strengthened by its relationship with its best pal, Ash.

FUN FACTS

Pikachu LOVES ketchup! Pikachu often tries to cover all its food with it before Ash steps in and takes the bottle away.

Pikachu chooses not to evolve, wanting to get stronger just as a Pikachu.

Pikachu is curious, smart and friendly. Like Ash, it is very competitive and determined and is often unwilling to give up in tough situations.

TOP POKÉMON

- Pikachu achieves many 'firsts' for Ash as a Trainer. Not only was Pikachu Ash's first Pokémon, but it was also the first to activate its ability, to be Gigantamaxed and to use Z-Moves and Dynamax.

- Pikachu always stays out of its Poké Ball and can often be seen riding around on Ash's head or shoulder.

- Pikachu is one of Ash's strongest and most dependable Pokémon. Pikachu often takes on the role of leader with Ash's other Pokémon.

Watch out! Pikachu can sometimes paralyse opponents with its static ability if they make direct contact during battle.

STATS

HEIGHT: 1' 04" (40 cm)
WEIGHT: 13 lbs (5.9 kg)
ABILITY: Static

HOW ASH AND PIKACHU MET

The story of how these two Pokémon heroes met is now the stuff of legend!

When a child turns ten, they can obtain their Pokémon licence and choose their first partner Pokémon from the local professor in the region. In the Kanto region, the three first partner choices are Charmander, Bulbasaur and Squirtle.

On the morning Ash was supposed to choose, he overslept. He ran to Professor Oak's lab while still dressed in his pyjamas!

Ash burst into the lab, and upon discovering that all three Pokémon had already been claimed, he pleaded with Professor Oak to give him any Pokémon. Luckily Oak had just one left ... Pikachu.

Things didn't start off well between Ash and Pikachu. Pikachu refused to go into its Poké Ball because it didn't trust Ash and shocked him several times. After Ash failed to catch a wild Pidgey because Pikachu refused to battle, Ash threw a rock in frustration and accidentally hit a Spearow. The Spearow started attacking Ash and then Pikachu, who shocked it, waking up the whole flock. To save Pikachu and escape the flock, Ash dived into a nearby waterfall. The two were later fished out by a young girl called Misty, who told Ash to take the injured Pikachu to the Pokémon Centre in Viridian City.

Having no other way to get there, Ash stole Misty's bike and pedalled quickly towards Viridian City, but the flock of Spearow were still in pursuit!

Ash lost control of the bike and crashed down the hill. He realised that Pikachu's condition was critical, so he begged Pikachu to go into its Poké Ball to protect it from the approaching Spearow. Pikachu could see that Ash cared for it, so it performed a powerful Thunder attack to drive the Spearow away. Unfortunately, it also destroyed Misty's bike. Whoops!

Pikachu learned to trust Ash and from then on, their friendship got stronger and stronger.

PALLET TOWN

Pallet Town is Ash's home town. He often returns here at the end of a big journey to relax and recharge. There might not be many big adventures to be had, but there are home-cooked meals, his bed ... and his mum, Delia.

Pallet Town is a quiet town – even the centre is small and sleepy. It is surrounded by beautiful rolling hills and fields. Located in the south-west of the Kanto region, it is not far to a river, a mountain and even a rocky valley. It is the home town of many Pokémon Trainers, including Professor Oak.

IMPORTANT LOCATIONS

PROFESSOR OAK'S LAB

Professor Oak and his assistant, Tracey, live and work in a complex on top of a hill. Behind Oak's home and laboratory is a huge ranch, which has ample room for lots of Pokémon to run free. The ranch has different environments to support all types of Pokémon. When Ash has a complete team of six Pokémon with him already, any further catches are transported to the ranch.

ASH'S HOUSE

Ash's house is located on an unpaved road in a quiet neighbourhood. It is a very peaceful place. When Ash is away on his Pokémon adventures, his mum, Delia, keeps busy with her garden and visiting her friend, Professor Oak. Delia has a Mr. Mime who helps her out with the chores.

THE XANADU NURSERY

This nursery is a large greenhouse very close to Pallet Town. Ash's mother, Delia, goes there often for plants for her garden. It is home to a flower which contains Stun Spore.

PROFESSOR OAK

Professor Samuel Oak is the regional professor for the Kanto region. He serves as a mentor and friend to Ash, giving him advice as he goes on his Pokémon journey. He and Delia often travel together to visit Ash on his adventures.

Professor Oak is a world-famous Pokémon researcher. He mainly studies the behaviour of Pokémon and their interactions with the human community. He's published his research extensively and he is credited with a lot of the information that people know about Pokémon, particularly in the Kanto region. All the data and research that he's collected over the years helped him build his greatest invention ever – the Pokédex.

Kanto Pokédex

Sinnoh Pokédex

Kalos Pokédex

Unova Pokédex

Johto Pokédex

Hoenn Pokédex

POETRY

Professor Oak loves to write poetry, in particular poems called senryū, which are Japanese short form poems of three lines with 15 to 17 syllables.

Some Professor Oak poetic classics:

*Put your fighting faith
In Starmie, to make sure that
You're safe from harm-y!*

*Blastoise fight or hide
Away, to fight again
Some other day.*

The Pokédex is a portable tool for Pokémon Trainers. It gives information about any new Pokémon they find, so long as it already exists in its database.

WELCOME TO THE ...
KANTO REGION

The Kanto region is the first area of the Pokémon world Ash visits and explores. It is located to the east of the Johto region – these are the only two Pokémon regions that are connected by land. The Kanto-Johto land mass is south of the Sinnoh region.

The ten major towns and cities in the Kanto region are named after colours, with the exception of Pallet Town, although the word 'palette' refers to a range of colours. All of the cities, of which Saffron City is the largest, can be found in the centre of the region, with close access to nearly every environment – sea, mountains, forests and plains. The Kanto region has a large bay in the centre which opens to the sea in the south-west.

BADGES ASH WON

Ash starts his journey to becoming a Pokémon Champion by winning badges in the Kanto region gyms. In order to enter the Indigo Conference League, Ash has to win eight badges.

Gym Leader:
Brock
Pewter City Gym
Type: Rock

BOULDER

Gym Leader:
Misty
Cerulean City Gym
Type: Water

CASCADE

Gym Leader:
Lt. Surge
Vermilion City Gym
Type: Electric

THUNDER

Gym Leader:
Sabrina
Saffron City Gym
Type: Psychic

MARSH

Gym Leader:
Erika
Celadon City Gym
Type: Grass

RAINBOW

Gym Leader:
Koga
Fuchsia City Gym
Type: Poison

SOUL

Gym Leader:
Blaine
Cinnabar Island Gym
Type: Fire

VOLCANO

Gym Leader:
Giovanni
Viridian City Gym
Type: Ground

EARTH

COMPETITIONS

Ash is not someone to shy away from a new challenge, adventure or competition, so he finds himself signing up for different competitions as he travels the region.

P1 GRAND PRIX · WINNER
Ash entered his Primape into the P1 Grand Prix – a competition for Fighting types. The final battle was against Team Rocket's Hitmonlee. Primape performed a Seismic Toss to win the match.

BIG P RACE · WINNER
The race to determine the best Pokémon on the Laramie Ranch. Lara, who planned to compete on her Ponyta, had injured her arm, so Ash rode in her place. Ponyta evolved into Rapidash to win by a nostril!

To read more about the details of each of Ash's Kanto gym battles, turn to pages 28 to 31.

ASH'S CATCHES

PIKACHU

TYPE:
Electric

Originally a wild Pichu, Pikachu eventually found its way to Professor Oak, where Ash obtained it as his first Pokémon. Pikachu is very powerful and the perfect partner for an aspiring Pokémon Master like Ash.

CATERPIE / METAPOD / BUTTERFREE

TYPE:
Bug / Flying

Butterfree was the first Pokémon Ash caught in the wild. It fought bravely as a Caterpie then as a Metapod. As a Butterfree, it helped a swarm of other wild Butterfree escape capture, and Ash set it free to be with its own kind.

PIDGEOTTO / PIDGEOT

TYPE:
Normal / Flying

Ash captured Pidgeot as a Pidgeotto, and it remained one of Ash's most loyal Pokémon for a long time. Eventually, after Pidgeot saved a flock of wild Pidgey from Team Rocket, Ash let it go so it could rejoin its family in the wild.

BULBASAUR

TYPE:
Grass / Poison

Bulbasaur does not want to evolve but is still very effective during battle. It once defeated a whole herd of Exeggutor single-handedly! Bulbasaur has also saved Ash, his friends and other Pokémon a number of times from Team Rocket.

CHARMANDER / CHARMELEON / CHARIZARD

TYPE:
Fire / Flying

Charizard is one of Ash's strongest Pokémon and he has used it in many battles. It wasn't always the most obedient Pokémon, testing Ash's patience as an overconfident Charmeleon, but eventually they learned to work together.

All great Pokémon Trainers need to catch and train a variety of Pokémon to become a champion. These are the Pokémon Ash caught in the Kanto region.

SQUIRTLE

TYPE:
Water

Like Pikachu and Bulbasaur, Squirtle has no interest in evolving. It is a small but feisty Pokémon. Squirtle defeated May's Electabuzz despite a type disadvantage. It also beat Brandon's Ninjask in the Battle Pyramid.

KRABBY / KINGLER

TYPE:
Water

Kingler is the only one of Ash's Pokémon to win a full league match by itself. As a Krabby, Kingler defeated Mandi's Exeggutor in the first round of the Pokémon Indigo League. Krabby spectacularly evolved to Kingler during this battle.

MANKEY / PRIMEAPE

TYPE:
Fighting

Ash met Primeape as a Mankey but captured it after it evolved. It was initially disobedient and had a bad temper, but eventually grew to trust and respect Ash. Primeape was able to defeat Team Rocket single-handedly at the P1 Grand Prix.

MUK

TYPE:
Poison

Muk doesn't feature in Ash's team very often and can usually be found causing havoc in Oak's lab. Though he smells rancid, Muk just wants to give everyone a big hug. Muk defeated Jeanette's Bellsprout during the Indigo League.

TAUROS (X 30!)

TYPE:
Normal

Ash caught 30 Tauros in the Safari Zone using Safari Balls. Tauros defeated Drake's Venusaur, battled Gary's Nidoqueen and was part of the team Ash assembled against Anabel's Alakazam and Metagross, but it didn't win.

MISTY

A chance encounter with Ash, when he borrowed or stole (depending on your point of view) Misty's bike, changed the course of her life. Misty is a confident, smart person who isn't afraid to stand up for things she believes to be right. She and her three sisters, Daisy, Violet and Lily – 'The Sensational Sisters' – run the Cerulean City Gym. In order to separate herself from her sisters, Misty sets off to become the greatest Water-type Pokémon Trainer ever. Like Ash, she is determined to be the best.

MEETING ASH

While Misty was fishing one day, she spotted Ash and his injured Pikachu running away from an angry flock of Spearow. She snagged both of them on the end of her fishing line when they ended up in the river. Misty directed them to the Pokémon Centre in Viridian City for treatment. Ash 'borrowed' Misty's bike to get Pikachu there more quickly. Later on, when Pikachu faced the flock, his Thunder Shock fried Misty's bike to a crisp. Misty eventually joined Ash on his adventure so she could make sure he would give her another bike.

FACTS

- The three things that disgust her the most are carrots, peppers and Bug-type Pokémon.

- She used to be afraid of Gyarados after one tried to eat her as a baby. She faced her fear by bravely befriending an angry Gyarados at the Cerulean City Gym.

- Misty eventually returns to the Cerulean City Gym and makes a name for herself as a great gym leader.

BROCK

Brock is an aspiring Pokémon doctor and breeder from Pewter City. Before meeting Ash, he was the gym leader at Pewter City Gym – the Rock-type gym – and was the first gym leader that Ash challenged. Brock looked after his nine younger siblings and the responsibility took its toll on Brock, leaving him unable to pursue his own dreams. When his Dad returned, Brock jumped at the chance to go travelling with Ash and explore the things he was interested in.

Brock is noticeably more mature, wise and level-headed than Ash and their travel companions, and often acts as the voice of reason during their arguments. He is the go-to man when it comes to information about where they are, battle strategies and Pokémon-Trainer relationships. He rarely takes part in battles himself, preferring to watch from the sidelines so he can learn and gain more knowledge about Pokémon.

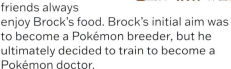

He is famous for his domestic skills, like sewing and most importantly, cooking – Ash and all their friends always enjoy Brock's food. Brock's initial aim was to become a Pokémon breeder, but he ultimately decided to train to become a Pokémon doctor.

FACTS

- He is the only friend to travel with Ash across multiple regions.

- He can tell all the Officer Jennys and Nurse Joys apart from each other.

TEAM ROCKET

No adventure would be complete without a villainous team trying to thwart the heroes' every move, would it? It's time to meet Team Rocket.

Team Rocket is based in the Kanto and Johto regions, with a small outpost in the Sevii Islands. It is a villainous organisation whose ultimate goal is to take over the world using Pokémon.

THE TRIO

'Team Rocket is blasting off aagggaaaiiinnn!'
The members of Team Rocket that Ash encounters constantly on his journey are the hapless trio of Jessie, James and Meowth. They hatch elaborate plans to capture Pokémon, but they always fail due to their own incompetence. They become obsessed with the idea that catching Ash's Pikachu would give them credit with their boss, Giovanni.

JESSIE

Jessie isn't always the best at controlling her emotions if she feels someone is insulting her. She gets quite angry when their missions fail, even though this happens regularly, because she is passionate and dedicated to getting it right for Team Rocket, and for James and Meowth. Both her teammates describe her as one of the strongest people they know.

She seems to have a special love of snake-like Pokémon – she has both an Arbok and a Seviper. Jessie has expressed a preference for Poison-type Pokémon too. Although she isn't very good at stealing Pokémon, Jessie eventually becomes a highly accomplished performer and a Master Class semi-finalist.

JESSIE'S KANTO REGION POKÉMON
Ekans / Arbok

MEOWTH

Meowth might seem to be devious and ambitious at first, but the Scratch Cat Pokémon is also an idealist. Its life goal is to please the big boss, because it is extremely jealous that Giovanni's Persian is 'top cat' instead of Meowth.

Most Pokémon only commit evil when ordered to do so, but Meowth often shows that it is very capable and willing to commit horrible deeds on its own. Meowth is highly motivated by self-interest and greed.

Meowth is the only known Pokémon to be able to talk. It mastered human speech to impress a Meowth called Meowsie, but was left rejected and heartbroken. Meowth recognises itself as a Pokémon, but often feels stuck between the Pokémon and human worlds, never truly fitting into either.

JAMES

James is the only child of millionaires, and this comfortable upbringing gave him the time to become well versed in Pokémon Haiku, Pokémon Orienteering and PokéRinger, among other activities.

Team Rocket offered him an escape from his family's demands and expectations. He has loved Pokémon since childhood. When he left home, his loyal Growlithe, Growlie, stayed behind to look after his parents. James often finds himself going along with Jessie and Meowth's schemes, even though the results never go in his favour.

JAMES'S KANTO REGION POKÉMON
Koffing / Weezing, Growlithe, Magikarp, Weepinbell / Victreebel

PROTECT YOUR POKÉMON!

While at the Pokémon Centre in Vermilion City, Ash heard about a powerful gym leader named Lt. Surge. It was obvious that very few Trainers were tough enough to defeat him, but Ash was determined to win a badge. Pikachu was reluctant to face Surge's mighty Raichu, but the battle commenced. Very quickly Ash realised Pikachu couldn't withstand Raichu's stronger and more powerful attacks, but when Ash tried to recall Pikachu, it refused. Raichu severely injured Pikachu using a Mega Punch. Although they were defeated, Ash was

just relieved to find out Pikachu was going to be okay. From then on, Ash realised that as a good Trainer, his responsibility was to protect his Pokémon, even if that meant losing a battle.

DON'T BE STUBBORN

It's a classic moment: the Metapod v Metapod epic showdown. In Ash's battle against Samurai, the two Metapod were too evenly matched. The battle went on too long and only came to an end when a Beedril swarm appeared. Ash learned not to stubbornly stay in a battle. Sometimes it's best for everyone to call it a draw.

SHARE THE WORLD

Ash knows it's important to live and share the world alongside the Pokémon. Ash and his friends once stumbled accidentally upon the Hidden Village, a place where injured Pokémon could go to rest and recover from injury

in safety. They knew they had to help protect it from poachers like Team Rocket!

> **'I wanna be the very best, like no one ever was …!'**
> In the Kanto region, Ash was just starting on his Pokémon adventure, and he had a lot to learn about himself and what it takes to be a good Pokémon Trainer. Here are some of the lessons Ash learned.

TO EVOLVE OR NOT?

This is a big question in the Pokémon world; should you evolve your Pokémon? Ash encountered some Trainers that forced Evolution as a quick way to get a more powerful Pokémon. This method may not have given those Pokémon the chance to develop their agility. When Ash was offered a Thunder Stone for Pikachu, he decided he would always leave it up to his Pokémon to decide if they want to evolve. Ash's Bulbasaur resisted evolving into an Ivysaur during the Evolution festival despite a lot of pressure from the other Pokémon. Ash supported his friend and said that if it does not want to evolve then no one can force it to do so.

BE A KIND TRAINER

Ash learned a lot about being a Pokémon Trainer from the other Trainers he met along the way. He discovered that not all Trainers treat their Pokémon properly. For example, Ash's Charmander had been abandoned in the rain by its original Trainer who thought it was too weak. Ash was horrified that anyone would treat their Pokémon like this, and so he went out of his way to heal Charmander and keep it safe. When its original Trainer tried to return it to its Poké Ball, Charmander hit it away and instead became one of Ash's Pokémon.

ALWAYS PUT YOUR POKÉMON FIRST

Ash learned very early on in his journey about how important it was to support his Pokémon's interests over his own. During the Butterfree mating season, Ash's Butterfree struggled to find a partner. Brock even gave Butterfree a yellow scarf so it stood out, but it still garnered no interest. Things changed though, when Team Rocket tried to catch all the Butterfree in a giant net. Ash's Butterfree bravely battled to help free the whole swarm, and this act of heroism attracted a pink admirer! Ash knew that his Butterfree would only be happy with a mate at its side, so he bid farewell to his friend. Butterfree was the first wild Pokémon Ash ever caught, and the first he released back into the wild.

TRAINER TALES

Ash collects many stories as he travels around the Pokémon world. Here are some of the interesting things that happen on his adventures in the Kanto region.

1 ASH CATCHES HIS FIRST POKÉMON

Catching your first Pokémon in the wild is always a big moment for any aspiring Pokémon Trainer. Ash caught a Caterpie in Viridian Forest. He didn't even battle it to weaken it, he just threw a Poké Ball at it!

2 THE GANG ARE SHIPWRECKED

Team Rocket tricked Ash and his friends on to a ship by telling them they'd won a luxury cruise. Jessie and James attempted to steal all of the gang's Pokémon, but their battle was interrupted by the onset of a massive storm. Ash and his friends, along with the dastardly Team Rocket, ended up in the water under attack from a group of Magikarp! They had to band together to make it ashore to a mysterious island.

3 TORNADO TROUBLE

Stranded on the unknown island, Ash, his friends and Team Rocket were then attacked by some terrifying Gyarados. The group was swept up in a tornado and separated across the island. Pikachu, Squirtle, Charmander and Bulbasaur were left alone and had to fend for themselves. Ash's other Pokémon believed Ash had abandoned them, but Pikachu didn't give up hope – Ash would never leave them. And, of course, it was right!

4 GIANT TENTACRUEL VERSUS HOTEL

In Porta Vista, a hotel was being built out in the ocean, over a coral reef. A HUGE Tentacruel and a shoal of Tentacool started rampaging the city, in an act of revenge against the humans who were destroying their ocean home. The humans and their Pokémon fought back, but the Tentacruel was too powerful. It captured Meowth to use as a puppet so it could speak. It thought humans were cruel and that Pokémon should not fight with them, and it destroyed the hotel. Pikachu passionately tried to reason with Tentacruel, as did Misty. She told Tentacruel they were sorry. The Tentacruel blasted the developer into the air and then returned to the sea with the army of Tentacool. Phew!

5 PIKA PIKA PIKA PIKA PIKA PIKA PIKA ...

While travelling deep into a forest with Brock and Misty, Ash and Pikachu discovered a large group of wild Pikachu. Ash watched as his Pikachu played happily, fitting in with its own kind. Pikachu continued to spend the day with the wild Pokémon, with Ash and his friends keeping a careful distance. Ash was sad knowing he should leave his best Pokémon pal with its new family. But when Team Rocket attacked, and Ash saved everyone, Pikachu knew it belonged with its heroic friend. Pika Pika!

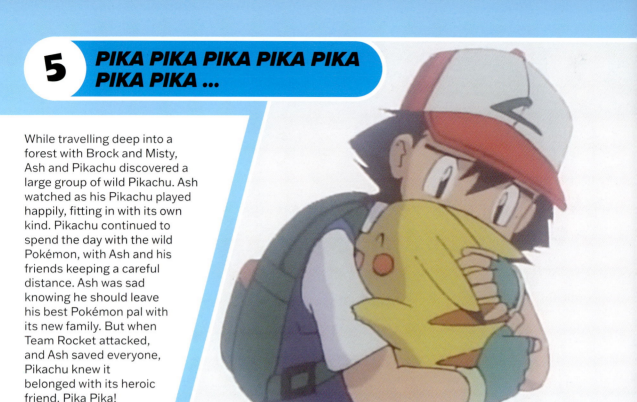

6 A SLEEPY CHARIZARD

After Charmander evolved into a Charmeleon, it developed a sassy attitude and didn't want to listen to Ash any more, believing it had the superior skill level. Ash continued to struggle with this for a long time, and it only got more difficult when it evolved again into the huge and mighty Charizard. Charizard did battle, but on its own terms – and it embarrassed Ash many times, most notably when it refused to fight against Ritchie's Sparky in the Indigo League match. Charizard fell asleep on the field, and so Ash forfeited the match.

7 THE EGG AND TOGEPI

After finding a mysterious egg in Grampa Canyon, the friends fought over who got to keep it. Ash found the egg, but it was Brock who looked after it before it hatched. Even Meowth lovingly looked after the egg after Team Rocket stole it. It was, however, Misty who was there when it hatched a Togepi. To settle things, Meowth, Brock, Ash and Misty battled for the new Pokémon. Even though Ash won the battle tournament, Togepi chose Misty, as she was the first person Togepi saw when it hatched.

8 JIGGLYPUFF'S SCRIBBLES

Ash and his friends were followed throughout their adventures in the Kanto region by a Jigglypuff intent on performing its trademark song. Unfortunately, the song always ended up putting its audience to sleep. This angered Jigglypuff, who then doodled all over the faces of those who had fallen asleep.

BATTLE BREAKDOWN

THE KANTO REGION GYM

PEWTER CITY GYM

BOULDER BADGE

The first time Ash challenged Brock, Ash had to surrender to save Pikachu, who was at a serious disadvantage against Rock-type Onix. This was Ash's first loss as a Trainer.

BATTLE 1

GEODUDE* V PIDGEOTTO

CERULEAN CITY GYM

CASCADE BADGE

The gym leaders, the Sensational Sisters (Misty's sisters), were too tired to battle, but Misty didn't want Ash to just be handed the Cascade Badge. She intended to battle him instead!

BATTLE 1

STARYU* V BUTTERFREE

VERMILLION CITY GYM

THUNDER BADGE

Lt. Surge is a fierce and intimidating gym leader. He used Pikachu's evolved form, Raichu, in the battle. He had forced Raichu to evolve too quickly, so even though it was the more powerful Pokémon, it didn't have the skills to win.

BATTLE 1

RAICHU* V PIKACHU

SAFFRON CITY GYM

MARSH BADGE

Saffron City Gym is run by what appeared to be a little girl. She turned out to be a very powerful but cruel Trainer named Sabrina with psychic abilities, known as the 'Master of Psychic-type Pokémon'.

BATTLE 1

KADABRA* V PIKACHU

Winning in the Kanto region gyms marks the start of Ash's Pokémon journey to become a champion. Let's break down each gym battle.

* winner
** winner after a match forfeit
*** interrupted battle

BATTLE 2

 **GEODUDE**

V

 **PIKACHU***

BATTLE 3

 **ONIX****

V

PIKACHU

Brock gave Ash the Boulder Badge for being kind.

BATTLE 2

 STARMIE

V

 **PIDGEOTTO*****

Ash and Misty's battle was never finished, but her sisters awarded Ash the badge for saving their gym.

Pikachu did not want to battle his friend, Misty.

BATTLE 2

 **RAICHU**

V

 PIKACHU*

After the first battle, Pikachu was offered the Thunder Stone to evolve – Pikachu refused.

Pikachu used Agility to win.

BATTLE 2

 KADABRA

V

 **HAUNTER****

Sabrina forfeited because she and Kadabra were laughing too hard at Haunter.

Ash was pleased to leave this spooky gym!

CELADON CITY GYM

RAINBOW BADGE

Ash was rude to a perfume shop owner in Celadon and was blacklisted all over town, including the gym. So Ash enlisted Team Rocket to help him. They dressed him up as a girl, and called him Ashley. The ruse worked ... until Pikachu rumbled him!

BATTLE 1

 V

TANGELA*   BULBASAUR

FUCHSIA CITY GYM

SOUL BADGE

This gym was a hidden ninja's lair! After he encountered a series of traps, Ash was challenged by a ninja warrior Trainer. The gym leader was the warrior's older brother, Koga.

BATTLE 1

 V

VENOMOTH*   PIDGEOTTO

CINNABAR ISLAND GYM

VOLCANO BADGE

In order to find this gym, Ash and his friends were tasked with solving riddles they received from a mysterious man, who turned out to be the gym leader, Blaine.

BATTLE 1   **BATTLE 2**

 V  V

NINETALES*   SQUIRTLE   RHYDON***   CHARIZARD

VIRIDIAN CITY GYM

EARTH BADGE

Giovanni, the gym leader of Viridian City, is also the boss of Team Rocket. Giovanni was not there when Ash arrived, so he had to battle Jessie and James instead.

BATTLE 1

 V

MACHAMP*   SQUIRTLE

BATTLE 2

 **WEEPINBELL** V  **CHARMANDER***

BATTLE 3

 **GLOOM*** V  **CHARMANDER**

BATTLE 4

 **GLOOM** V  **PIKACHU*****

BATTLE 2

 **VENOMOTH** V **CHARMANDER*****

This battle was interrupted by Team Rocket, who were beaten by Misty's Psyduck using Disable and Confusion.

BATTLE 3

 **GOLBAT** V  **CHARMANDER***

BATTLE 3

 **RHYDON** V  **PIKACHU***

BATTLE 4

 **MAGMAR**** V  **PIKACHU**

BATTLE 5

 **MAGMAR** V  **CHARIZARD***

BATTLE 2

 **KINGLER*** V  **BULBASAUR**

BATTLE 3

 **RHYDON** V  **PIDGEOTTO***

BATTLE 4

 **ARBOK AND WEEZING** V  **PIKACHU***

THE INDIGO LEAGUE CONFERENCE

The first four rounds of this conference are 3-on-3 battles in separate stadiums, on different battlefields: Rock, Grass, Water and Ice. Each competitor must win on all four battlefields. The final 16 battles are held on a standard field in Indigo Stadium. These matches are 3-on-3, with opponents decided by each Trainer fishing for a Magikarp with a number on it. From the final eight battles onwards, they are 6-on-6.

* winner
** winner after a match forfeit
*** interrupted battle

MATCH 1 Mandi v Ash

BATTLEFIELD TYPE: Water

BATTLE 1 — EXEGGUTOR V KRABBY*

Krabby's first-ever battle! It looked like nothing would beat Exeggutor's Whirlwind, which created a massive whirlpool, but Krabby took the win with Leer and Stomp moves.

BATTLE 2 — SEADRA V KINGLER*

Krabby evolved into the much stronger Kingler. Seadra put up a good defence using Agility, but Kingler took it out with Water Gun, Bubble and Crabhammer.

BATTLE 3 — GOLBAT V KINGLER*

Mandi tried to end the battle by using her Golbat's Mega Drain, but Ash took his first Indigo League victory by instructing Kingler to use its Hyper Beam move!

MATCH 2 Red Trainer v Ash
BATTLEFIELD TYPE: Rock

BATTLE 1

NIDORINO V SQUIRTLE*

Nidorino started the attack, but Squirtle did a Withdraw into its shell and rolled away. It wasn't retreating though. It returned with Water Gun to win!

MATCH 3 Pete Pebbleman v Ash
BATTLEFIELD TYPE: Ice

BATTLE 1

CLOYSTER V KINGLER*

Pete played this battle cautiously, instructing his Cloyster to retreat from Kingler's Crabhammer. But Ash was relentless, and Kingler persisted to victory.

BATTLE 2

ARCANINE* V KINGLER

Arcanine's big move here was Dragon Rage. sweeping Kingler into an icy twister. Ash was forced to recall his injured Pokémon and concede the battle and the win.

BATTLE 3

ARCANINE V PIKACHU*

Pete's strategy was to melt the ice field, to slow down Pikachu. But Pikachu used it to its advantage, using a water-enhanced Thunderbolt to defeat Arcanine.

MATCH 4 Jeanette Fisher v Ash

BATTLEFIELD TYPE: Grass

BATTLE 1

BEEDRILL V BULBASAUR*

Beedrill and Bulbasaur seemed evenly matched with both dodging the other's attack. Finally, Bulbasaur used Leech Seed to drain Beedrill's energy and win.

BATTLE 2

SCYTHER V BULBASAUR*

Jeanette ordered Scyther to use Double Team. Bulbasaur took some huge hits before Ash realised he should take aim at all three Scythers.

BATTLE 3

BELLSPROUT* V BULBASUAR

Bellsprout absorbed the energy from Bulbasaur's attacks and redirected them, eventually knocking Bulbasaur out.

BATTLE 4

BELLSPROUT* V PIKACHU

Bellsprout was unaffected by Pikachu's electric attacks – its roots kept it grounded. Pikachu tried to kick and punch Bellsprout but was knocked out.

BATTLE 5

BELLSPROUT V MUK*

Finally, Ash sent out Muk who absorbed all the grass attacks Bellsprout threw at it. With this battle win, Ash advanced to the final 16.

FINAL MATCH!

MATCH 5 Ritchie v Ash

BATTLEFIELD TYPE: Indigo Stadium

Ash was late after being held up by Team Rocket's exploits but the friends had promised each other that this would be the best battle they'd ever had.

BATTLE 1 — BUTTERFREE* V SQUIRTLE

This quick match started with Butterfree and Squirtle exchanging blows and attacks until Butterfree defeated Squirtle using Sleep Powder. Zzzz.

BATTLE 2 — BUTTERFREE V PIKACHU*

Despite having just battled Team Rocket, Pikachu told Ash it was ready. It launched a Double-Edge attack and a Thunderbolt to win. Pikachu was visibly tired.

BATTLE 3 — CHARMANDER* V PIKACHU

Charmander used Flamethrowers against Pikachu, who used its speed and agility to dodge them. Worn out by all the battles, Pikachu could no longer keep up.

BATTLE 4 — CHARMANDER V CHARIZARD*

Left with no other choice of Pokémon for this battle, Ash sent out his disobedient Charizard, who won the battle with a mighty Flamethrower.

BATTLE 5 — PIKACHU** V CHARIZARD

Charizard was offended by this match-up, so stomped on the ground to knock over Pikachu. It then lost interest and laid down to take a nap. Ash was eliminated.

ORANGE ISLANDS

The Orange Islands are a group of 24 tropical islands, located south of the Kanto and Johto regions. Many Pokémon Trainers come to the islands to participate in the Orange League, but its tropical climate attracts lots of tourists too.

All the Islands are named after types of oranges or citrus fruits. Kumquat Island is a luxurious resort with fantastic hotels, hot springs and pristine beaches. The group of seven small islands in the Grapefruit Archipelago supply nearly all the grapefruit for the world's regions. Sunburst Island is world-famous for its glass-blown works of art. The largest island is Mandarin Island, with the biggest city being the port of Troviopolis on the western side.

One big difference between the Orange Islands and the Kanto region mainland, is that the warmer climate affects the colour variation of certain Pokémon. For example, the Orange Islands Butterfree has a different wing pattern, and the Vileplume has different colouring on its flower.

BADGES ASH WON

Only four Orange League badges are required to participate in the championship competition, which is held on Pummelo Island. Unlike in other regions, the Orange League requires participants to complete challenges alongside the Orange gym leaders.

Gym Leader: Danny
Navel Island

Challenges:
Climb a mountain with no help from Pokémon, freeze a hot-water geyser, carve a sled out of ice and finally, race down the mountain to the beach.

SEA RUBY

Gym Leader: Rudy
Trovita Island

Challenges:
Knock down targets with Water Gun, three-round gym battle using three different Pokémon types.

SPIKE SHELL

Gym Leader: Cissy
Mikan Island

Challenges: Water Gun Match-up and Pokémon Wave Ride

CORAL EYE

Gym Leader: Luana
Kumquat Island

Challenges:
Double Battle

JADE STAR

A QUICK DELIVERY ...

Ash came to the Orange Islands because Professor Oak asked him to collect the mysterious GS Ball from Professor Ivy. But Ash couldn't resist the lure of competition and decided to stay and compete in the Orange League to gain some extra training and experience before the Indigo League.

To read more about the details of each of Ash's Orange Islands gym challenges, turn to pages 46 to 47.

ASH'S CATCHES

A new area to explore gave Ash the opportunity to capture new Pokémon! These are the Pokémon he caught in the Orange Islands.

LAPRAS

TYPE:
Water / Ice

Notable feats: Lapras was stranded on a beach on Tangelo Island when Ash found it. He gained its trust when it was kidnapped by Team Rocket, and Ash came to the rescue of Lapras and its family. Lapras would allow Ash, Misty and Tracey to ride on its back between islands. Lapras used its Ice Beam move to help Ash beat Cissy and her Blastoise in a Pokémon Wave Ride, which earned Ash his first Orange League badge.

SNORLAX

TYPE:
Normal

Notable feats: Ash found Snorlax eating everything in sight on the Seven Grapefruit Islands. Once it joined Ash's team, Snorlax got a lot of victories under its belt, including defeating Clair's Kingdra, Gary's Nidoqueen and Arcanine, Greta's Hariyama and Medicham. However, Ash couldn't use Snorlax in the Orange League final because it wouldn't wake up! Snorlax's Poké Ball was the only one of Ash's to ever break.

WHAT'S TEAM ROCKET UP TO?

Jesse, James and Meowth followed Ash over to the Orange Islands, determined to succeed in finally snatching Pikachu. What could go wrong?!

Since the trio had not caught any new Pokémon for their boss, Giovanni, he punished them by assigning them to Team Rocket's Dirigible Brigade, where their duty was to operate an airship. Little did they know that this was Giovanni's way of getting rid of them, as he had not repaired the ship for  decades. During a battle with Ash, Misty and Brock, Team Rocket were almost successful in stealing Pikachu, but suddenly the airship hit turbulence and they were blasted off!

When the trio landed on Golden Island, they were taken in by the locals, who immediately gave Meowth  food, attention and power over the island. The islanders worshipped the legendary 'Meowth of Bounty' and believed the trio's appearance on their island would fulfill their prophecy: that a Meowth would arrive during a full white moon and make them all rich using its Pay Day attack.

Meowth didn't know this move, so he was taken to a stadium to develop the technique through battle. Jessie and James were determined to be reunited with Meowth, so they showered the stadium in bottle caps to convince the crowd Meowth had performed the Pay Day move.

PROFESSOR IVY

Professor Felina Ivy is the young resident professor of the Orange Islands. She is known for being calm, friendly and passionate when talking about her scientific pursuits.

As the Orange Islands themselves are scattered, Professor Ivy's research takes her around to lots of different places. Her area of expertise is in how the regions and their climates affect a Pokémon's physiology. She looks at the different species' physical characteristics, their way of living, how they are arranged into types, their moves and abilities. She is an accomplished author and can also skilfully ride a Gyarados.

She lives on Valencia Island, where she is helped by her assistants, Charity, Hope and Faith – collectively known as the triplets. Ash's friend Brock also stayed and became a research assistant with the professor for a while when the friends travelled through the Orange Islands.

TRACEY SKETCHIT

Tracey loves Pokémon, but his goal in life isn't to become a Trainer or a breeder, instead he just wants to watch and observe Pokémon in order to learn everything about them.

Tracey really admires Professor Oak, so when a chance encounter with Ash happened, Tracey knew this was the way to meet his hero. He began travelling with Ash and Misty when they visited the Islands.

Tracey is a very gentle person, who has a hard time saying no to anyone. He is very focused on his quest to further his Pokémon knowledge, to the extent that he often misses what is happening around him. Once he even found himself wandering out on to a battlefield in an attempt to study the Pokémon more closely!

HOW TRACEY MET ASH

Ash was just about to battle three Trainers who had been mistreating an injured Lapras, when suddenly Tracey appeared and shouted at them all to stop. He wanted to measure and observe their Pokémon. He called the Pokémon of the three bad Trainers 'underdeveloped' but thought Pikachu looked very strong.

PROFESSOR OAK'S ASSISTANT

When he finally met his hero, Tracey was inspired by Ash's courage to ask Oak if he could be his assistant. Oak accepted, so now Tracey helps with Oak's research and cares for the Pokémon at the ranch.

FACTS

- Tracey has unnaturally good eyesight.

- In order to observe Pokémon undetected, Tracey approaches them from downwind, so they can't smell him.

- He changes his breathing rhythm to match the Pokémon's so they can't hear him either.

- He has the unique ability to know what move a Pokémon is going to use just by watching the way it acts.

HELP INJURED POKÉMON

When Ash ran into three Trainers being mean to an injured Lapras, he didn't think twice before jumping in to defend it. Ash went to great lengths to save and protect his Pokémon and he took the same approach to Pokémon that weren't his own. After its experience, Lapras was afraid of humans, and wouldn't take any medicine when offered. Ash tried a lot of things to make Lapras comfortable, including jumping into the pool with it, and later, saving it from Team Rocket. In the end, Lapras felt safe and comfortable around Ash and decided to join Ash's team.

APOLOGISE FOR YOUR MISTAKES

After defeating Team Rocket when they crashed Ash's celebration in Pallet Town, Pidgeotto was injured, so Ash took him to Professor Oak's lab. Ash apologised to Pidgeotto for letting him get hurt in the battle. It wasn't the right strategy and he had to take responsibility.

NEVER GIVE UP ON YOUR POKÉMON

Ash worked hard to repair his relationship with Charizard, which definitely took a lot of time and patience. When Ash battled a Trainer called Tag on Cleopatra Island, Charizard was defeated by a Poliwrath. This loss knocked Charizard's confidence as it realised it wasn't as powerful as it thought. It was left weak and injured, and Ash did all he could to help. As Ash did this, he told Charizard that he was going to get better as a Trainer in the hope that he and Charizard could continue on side by side. From this moment, the pair started to work together as a team.

Ash initially visited the Orange Islands on an errand, but ended up staying to compete in the Orange League. There's no adventure for Ash without learning some important lessons along the way. Here are some of the things that Ash learned in the Orange Islands.

BELIEVE IN YOUR POKÉMON

During the battle against Rudy's Starmie for the Spike Shell Badge, Squirtle gained a lot of strength from Ash's belief in him. As Misty shouted at Ash, 'You're the only one who can bring out Squirtle's real power!' Squirtle channelled this belief into learning a new move, Hydro Pump, and then defeated Starmie.

LISTEN TO YOUR FRIENDS

During the tense first battle against Drake, Ash ignored advice from Misty who urged him to switch out Pikachu. Luckily keeping Pikachu on the field turned out to be the correct call, but he definitely won this battle the hard way.

LOVE IS A STRENGTH

During his battles on the Orange Islands, there were many moments when Ash's love for his Pokémon gave them extra strength, whether that was to stand back up after being knocked down, or believing that their attacks would be strong and accurate. During the battle with Drake, Ash's strongest Pokémon were the ones that had been with him the longest, whereas Tauros, who had been living at the Oak Corral this whole time, was not as successful.

TRAINER TALES

This mysterious set of islands provides Ash with many adventures and lessons. Here are some of the interesting moments from his journey through the Orange Islands.

1 PIDGEOT'S CALLING

When Ash and the gang left Pallet Town for the Orange Islands, they ran into a flock of angry Spearow. They were led by a Fearow, and not just any Fearow: the one that Ash threw a rock at when it was a Spearow at the beginning of his journey. And it remembered. The Fearow and flock of Spearow were in a territory war with the Pidgey and Pidgeotto, and Ash's Pidgeotto stepped up to lead and protect the flock. The battle with Fearow caused Pidgeotto to evolve into Pidgeot. After it defeated Fearow with the help of the rest of the Pidgey flock, Ash knew that Pidgeot needed to stay to look after the flock. The two shared an emotional goodbye.

2 CATCHING SNORLAX

When the friends visited the seven Grapefruit Islands, they discovered that someone had been stealing from the grapefruit harvest. The culprit turned out to be a hungry, hungry Snorlax. Jigglypuff had also been spotted on the island. To stop Snorlax, they built a stage for Jigglypuff to coax it to sing and send Snorlax to sleep. As Jigglypuff started to sing, Pikachu managed a Thunder attack on the drowsy Snorlax. Ash was able to catch it … right before falling asleep!

3 PIKACHU AND CHARIZARD FALL OUT!

During their Double Battle match with Luana, Pikachu and Charizard fell out. Charizard stomped and it knocked Pikachu over and Pikachu got cross. There was no way that Ash could win the Jade Star Badge if his team were fighting each other instead of their opponent! After Charizard barbecued Pikachu, Pikachu refused to battle alongside Charizard. But when Pikachu was hit with a Body Slam from Marowak, Charizard caught Pikachu with its wing to cushion the blow. From then on, Pikachu and Charizard fought together as a team and won the match.

4 GOODBYE TO BROCK

After meeting Professor Ivy on the Orange Islands, Brock was so impressed by her research that he decided to stay behind and assist her. He wanted to learn more about Pokémon. But don't worry, this wasn't goodbye to Brock for long … He and Ash were friends to the end, and they were reunited when Ash went back home to Pallet Town. He was so surprised to see Brock in his mum's kitchen that Ash fell to the floor!

5 BATTLE OF THE RIVALS: GARY V ASH

This was Ash and Gary's first-ever Pokémon battle, despite being rivals from childhood. It was tense with two amazing Pokémon who battled well, but eventually Gary's Eevee was just too powerful for Ash's Pikachu and he won the battle. Both congratulated their Pokémon and Gary told Ash he did a great job, showing how far they'd both come as Trainers, and people, since they started their Pokémon journeys.

BATTLE BREAKDOWN

ORANGE ISLANDS GYM

MIKAN ISLAND GYM

CORAL EYE BADGE

The first challenge pits two Pokémon with water-shooting abilities against each other to knock down cans and flying discs. Seadra and Squirtle were evenly matched and the challenge ended in a draw.

WATER GUN CHALLENGE

 V

SEADRA | SQUIRTLE

NAVEL ISLAND GYM

SEA RUBY BADGE

Before the contests can even begin, Ash must climb up a mountain without the help of any Pokémon.

GEYSER FREEZING

 V

NIDOQUEEN* | LAPRAS

TROVITA ISLAND GYM

SPIKE SHELL BADGE

Rudy will only accept a challenge if first the challenger has their Pokémon knock down targets. Then the battle is a type-on-type battle, three Pokémon from each Trainer battling against another Pokémon of the same type.

ELECTRIC-TYPE BATTLE

 V

ELECTABUZZ* | PIKACHU

KUMQUAT ISLAND GYM

JADE STAR BADGE

In order to gain the gym's badge, challengers must use two of their Pokémon to defeat two of Luana's Pokémon in a Double Battle. As soon as one Pokémon from either team is unable to battle, the other Trainer is the winner.

DOUBLE POKÉMON BATTLE

 V

ALAKAZAM / MAROWAK | PIKACHU / CHARIZARD*

The Orange Islands Gym challenges are based on contests of skill, not battles. The philosophy is that Trainers must know all aspects of their Pokémon to win each round.

* winner
** winner after a match forfeit
*** interrupted battle

POKÉMON WAVE RIDE

To break the tie, Cissy challenges Ash to a race, where the Pokémon have to swim around a flag and back to the beach. Ash surfs Lapras to victory!

 **BLASTOISE** V  **LAPRAS***

ICE SCULPTING

 **PIKACHU, BULBASAUR AND CHARIZARD*** V  **MACHOKE, SCYTHER AND NIDOQUEEN**

ICE-SLEDGE RACE

Danny and Ash, along with their Pokémon, race down the mountain to the beach. It's a bumpy finish but a win for Ash and his team.

GRASS-TYPE BATTLE

 **EXEGGUTOR** V  **BULBASAUR***

WATER-TYPE BATTLE

 **STARMIE** V **SQUIRTLE***

Pikachu and Charizard don't work well together and it looks like Luana's Pokémon will be triumphant. But Pikachu jumps on to Charizard's back just in time to land a flying Thunderbolt move on their opponents, winning the challenge.

ORANGE LEAGUE FINALS

After he earned four Orange League badges, Ash travelled to Pummelo Island to face his greatest and most difficult battle yet. It was time to challenge the undefeated and seemingly unstoppable Supreme Gym Leader Drake in the Orange League Finals.

* winner
** double faint

BATTLE RULES

This was a 6-on-6 battle. When three of one Trainer's Pokémon were unable to battle, the field was changed. Drake cannot switch out his Pokémon, but the challenger can switch theirs out at any time.

BATTLEFIELD 1: Rock and Water

BATTLE 1

DITTO V PIKACHU*

Ditto opened the match by using Transform, turning itself into a Pikachu. Pikachu struck it with Thunder, only for the attack to be returned by Ditto. Too evenly matched, the pair fired similar moves at each other until Pikachu was able to get back up quickly and knock out Ditto with its tail.

BATTLE 2
ONIX V SQUIRTLE*

During the battle, Ash told Squirtle to get into the water. However, Onix caught Squirtle first, knocking it up into the air before holding it in Bind. Squirtle managed to counter by using Hydro Pump. Onix was unable to escape the water torrent and Squirtle finished the match with Skull Bash.

BATTLE 3
GENGAR* V TAUROS

No Pokémon has a type advantage against a Ghost type, so Ash decided to try beginner's luck by sending Tauros for its first battle. Tauros used Fissure, but Gengar jumped into the air to avoid the attack. Gengar then used Confuse Ray on Tauros, leaving Ash with no choice but to recall it.

BATTLE 4
GENGAR** V LAPRAS**

Ash then sent out Lapras. Gengar used Night Shade at the same time that Lapras used Ice Beam. The two attacks collided in mid-air before exploding and engulfing the entire stadium. When the smoke had cleared, both Gengar and Lapras had fainted from the impact.

BATTLE 5

VENUSAUR V TAUROS*

The desert battlefield proved tough for Tauros, with its moves being absorbed by the sand and its hooves unable to hold steady when attacked. Venusaur used a series of Vine Whips, a few of which hit Tauros but most were dodged. Finally, Tauros did the Take Down attack to knock Venusaur out.

BATTLE 6

ELECTABUZZ* V BULBASAUR

Drake opened the battle with a Thunder Shock from Electabuzz, but Bulbasaur just absorbed it and then countered with Razor Leaf. Bulbasaur did a Tackle, and Electabuzz struck at the same time with a Thunder Punch. Bulbasaur landed its attack but was knocked out by Electabuzz.

BATTLE 7

ELECTABUZZ V CHARIZARD*

Ash told Charizard to attack with Flamethrower, but Electabuzz jumped over the flames and countered quickly with a Thunder Punch. Charizard flew into the air and grabbed its opponent before it could attack with Thunderbolt and used Seismic Toss to defeat Electabuzz.

BATTLE 8

DRAGONITE* V CHARIZARD

Charizard opened with a Flamethrower, but Dragonite countered with Water Gun, cutting through the flames and hitting Charizard. Charizard flew into the air and Dragonite fired an Ice Beam, which Charizard dodged, but when Dragonite flew and fired an Ice Beam again, it hit Charizard's wing sending it into freefall. Dragonite then used Slam, crashing its opponent into the ground. Remarkably, Charizard got to its feet, and Ash told it to use Dragon Rage. Drake told Dragonite to do the same. The attacks collided throwing each Pokémon backwards. Dragonite was left dazed and Charizard fainted.

BATTLE 9

DRAGONITE V SQUIRTLE / TAUROS / PIKACHU*

Dragonite was severely weakened and Ash knew that none of his remaining Pokémon could take on Dragonite alone. He decided they should work together to tire Dragonite out. First out was Squirtle, who used Bubble and got a few hits on Dragonite before it was knocked out with Body Slam. Tauros was next up using Take Down, but Dragonite flew up and used Body Slam. Luckily the sand absorbed much of the power, but Dragonite then did a Thunder attack which knocked Tauros out. Last up, it was Pikachu, who used its tail as a spring to dodge Dragonite's attacks. Pikachu aimed a Thunderbolt to its head and Dragonite finally went down. Ash was the new champion of the Orange League!

WELCOME TO THE ...
JOHTO REGION

The Johto region is located to the west of the Kanto region, and together they form a joint land mass to the south of the Sinnoh region. You can travel between the two regions on a ship or a high-speed train. The Johto region has ten cities, with Goldenrod City being one of the largest cities in the world; so sprawling that even people who live there often get lost! Another famous landmark is the Whirl Islands; named after the dangerous whirlpools that surround them.

In ancient times, Ho-Oh, the Legendary Pokémon, lived in a tower in Ecruteak City until the war when the tower was burned down. The Legendary beasts, Entei, Raikou and Suicune, were created when the tower was destroyed. Now there are two towers in Ecruteak City: Bell Tower and Burned Tower, which were built to represent friendship and hope between Pokémon and people.

BADGES ASH WON

To qualify for Johto's Silver League, a Trainer must earn eight badges from either the Indigo or Silver Leagues. They allow a Trainer to battle the Elite Four at Kanto's Indigo Plateau.

Gym Leader:
Faulkner
Violet City Gym
Type: Flying

ZEPHYR

Gym Leader:
Bugsy
Azalea Town Gym
Type: Bug

HIVE

Gym Leader:
Whitney
Goldenrod City Gym
Type: Normal

PLAIN

Gym Leader:
Morty
Ecruteak City Gym
Type: Ghost

FOG

Gym Leader:
Chuck
Cianwood City
Type: Fighting

STORM

Gym Leader:
Jasmine
Olivine City Gym
Type: Ground

MINERAL

To read more about the details of each of Ash's Johto gym battles, turn to pages 66 to 69.

Gym Leader:
Pryce
Mahogany Town Gym
Type: Ice

GLACIER

Gym Leader:
Clair
Blackthorn City Gym
Type: Dragon

RISING

COMPETITIONS

Ash is always confident he'll win and the Johto region presented lots of opportunities for him to train and compete with his friends!

FIRE AND RESCUE GRAND PRIX – WINNER

Water-type Pokémon test how they work together as firefighters. Ash's Squirtle rejoined his Squirtle Squad and led them into the final against Team Wartortle! The Squirtles rescued a dummy from the fire in the quickest time and won!

EXTREME POKÉMON RACE – WINNER

Each Trainer puts one of their Pokémon in a collar with a lead and is pulled along the course on a skateboard, picking up an egg on the way. Ash used Bayleef and competed against Gary and his Arcanine. Ash and Bayleef won – it was a photo finish!

ASH'S CATCHES

A new region means new Pokémon for Ash to catch and get to know! Here are the Pokémon he caught in the Johto region.

HERACROSS

TYPE:
Bug / Fighting

Heracross was the first Pokémon Ash caught there. It is an eager but easily distracted Pokémon, especially if there's sap around! It was powerful in battle against Team Rocket, also defeating Gary's Magmar and Blastoise.

CHIKORITA / BAYLEEF

TYPE:
Grass

Chikorita showed courage when it went up against Ash's Charizard despite the overwhelming odds against it. Now evolved into Bayleef, it is a powerful battler, often using its vines to push into a jump in the air to avoid its opponent's moves.

CYNDAQUIL / QUILAVA

TYPE:
Fire

Cyndaquil is the baby of Ash's team. It started off quite weak and tired easily, but has excellent reflexes. Its Eruption move was enough to blast Team Rocket away. After it evolved into Quilava, it became very calm and serious.

TOTODILE

TYPE:
Water

Totodile is very happy. It often dances during its moves in battle. Totodile defeated Macy's Slugma during the Silver Conference. It also helped calm down the flames caused by Cyndaquil while fighting Team Rocket.

NOCTOWL

TYPE:
Normal / Flying

Noctowl was Ash's first Pokémon in the Johto region and is a silent flier, but it is quite small compared to other Noctowls. Although it is a Normal and Flying type, it also has psychic abilities that it uses to battle against Ghost-type Pokémon.

PROFESSOR ELM

Professor Elm is the professor for the Johto region. He lives in New Bark Town and specialises in Pokémon breeding. He is credited with discovering the existence of Pokémon eggs.

Everyone who knows Professor Elm thinks that he is sweet and kind-hearted. He is incredibly knowledgeable about Pokémon and he often gets into passionate discussions over theories. Whenever he is asked a question, he will give a long and detailed answer. He can get so focused on something, especially his research, that he forgets to do anything else and won't leave his lab for days. Another special interest of study for Professor Elm is unusual Pokémon abilities. He is the author of *A Brilliant Analysis of Hypersized Communicative Faculties of Pokémon*.

POKÉMON PRESERVATION COUNCIL

Professor Elm is the head of the Pokémon Preservation Council. He sent Ash on an errand to retrieve a stolen egg from the nearby Marine Pokémon Laboratory. The egg then hatched into Larvitar, which Ash and his friends eventually returned to its mother, Tyranitar.

CASEY

Casey meets Ash not long after picking up her first Pokémon, Chikorita, from Professor Elm. This over-confident novice Trainer is baseball mad and loves to win!

Casey is a diehard Electabuzz baseball team fan. Her favourite Pokémon are yellow-and-black striped, just like her beloved baseball team's uniform and she hopes one day to train an Electabuzz. She finds defeat difficult to deal with, but even when she's down, she's not out and her fighting spirit usually has her back up on her feet quickly.

HOW CASEY MET ASH

Ash made the mistake of insulting Casey's beloved team, so she challenged him to a battle. Ash agreed to a 3-on-3 battle, but he knew he wasn't going to need all three. Ash sent out Charizard to face her Pidgey, Rattata and Chikorita – a completely uneven match. Charizard didn't move a muscle and easily knocked out its three opponents. Casey ran away disappointed, but the loss didn't dampen her ambition for long.

WHAT'S TEAM ROCKET UP TO?

The most unlucky and incapable trio, Jessie, James and Meowth, follow Ash to the Johto region, where their schemes here get more elaborate and include more and more crazy tech and machinery. Will they finally succeed? No, the answer is no.

FOREST GRUMPS

The trio were attacked by a pack of Ursaring in the forest while attempting to steal Ash, Brock and Misty's Pokémon. The chaos caused the group to split up, leaving Jessie with Ash and Brock, and Misty with James and Meowth. To escape the raging Ursaring, they all agreed to work together. Jessie, James and Meowth got an insight into how 'the twerps' live.

But soon the temporary truce was over. Back to their old ways: Jessie and James tried to steal Pikachu, resulting in Team Rocket blasting off … AGAIN!

'HELPING' CHARIZARD

Just when you think that the trio is only focused on wrongdoing, they do something surprisingly thoughtful and kind. When Charizard was locked out of the training ground by its fellow Pokémon, Team Rocket felt unusually sympathetic and tried to help. Meowth knew how it felt to not be as strong as other Pokémon of your type. The trio attacked the training ground, forcing Charizard to defend it. The other Charizards saw its bravery and allowed it to join them.

WOBBUFFET

At the Pokémon Swap Meet, Jessie accidentally traded her Lickitung for Wobbuffet. She was devastated and didn't like Wobbuffet at all. It always burst out of its Poké Ball unannounced at the funniest moments or when Jessie called out another Pokémon for battle. She soon grew to love Wobbuffet though – it even got to join in the Team Rocket motto!

JESSIE AND BLISSEY

Blissey is an old friend of Jessie's from her days training as a Pokémon nurse, they even had matching BFF necklaces. They recognised each other immediately, but Jessie didn't want Blissey to suffer from being associated with an evil Team Rocket member and have it affect its reputation as a nurse. Jessie had her Lickitung and Arbok 'pretend' to attack Chancey to drive it away.

DELIBIRD

When the trio ran into a Team Rocket scout, she tried to recruit them. The system showed they were no longer members because they had been kicked out for owing too much money to Giovanni! The scout told them that they could get back in if they defeated a Trainer. They went up against Ash, again, and lost … again. The scout still allowed them back in Team Rocket, but to make sure they paid their debts, a Delibird was going to follow them around.

BATTLE FAIRLY

Soon after he first met Casey, Ash learned he shouldn't treat novice Trainers the same as more experienced opponents. When they battled, Casey had only just received her first Pokémon, and Ash easily won using his much stronger Charizard. Brock and Misty both got angry at Ash for being unfair in his choice of Pokémon. This issue arose again soon after, when Ash came across a young, wild Chikorita and he decided to bring out his Charizard to battle it. Despite the overwhelming odds, and an injury, Chikorita showed how brave, determined and stubborn it was.

EMOTIONAL BONDS ARE STRENGTH

When Ash first challenged Pryce, the Mahogany Gym Leader, to a gym battle, Pryce said no. He thought that Ash was too emotionally involved with his Pokémon. Pryce believed that to perform at the top of their ability, Pokémon must be tense and that friendship with their Trainer clouded judgment in battle. Pryce used to have a strong friendship with a Piloswine when he was younger, but after Pryce was badly burned in battle, Piloswine abandoned him. When Pryce watched as Ash and his Pokémon worked together in crisis, and when they reunited him with his beloved Piloswine, the bitterness in his heart melted away.

A new region brings new challenges, adventures and lessons for Ash as he continues to develop as a Pokémon Trainer. Here are some of the lessons that Ash learned in the Johto region.

BE COMPASSIONATE

One of Chikorita's favourite things to do was to celebrate with Ash by jumping into his arms for a cuddle. When it evolved into Bayleef, it went to hug Ash in the usual way, unaware of its now much larger size. Ash was hurt and scolded Bayleef, who ran away in tears. Ash felt terrible and ran to find Bayleef. He promised to be more considerate about its feelings, and Bayleef learned to express affection in a different way.

DAVID V GOLIATH

In his match against Janina's Steelix, Ash sent out Cyndaquil, who had a type advantage against Steel, but was small, young and definitely the 'baby' of Ash's Pokémon. 'Steelix may be bigger and stronger,' Ash told it, 'But you have the heart of a Fire Pokémon!' Ash's belief and confidence in his Cyndaquil, along with his tactics, helped Cyndaquil feel confident enough to take on such a large opponent, get back up when it was injured and win in a true David versus Goliath take-down.

THE WILL TO WIN ISN'T ALWAYS ENOUGH

An over-confident Ash entered into a Grass Tournament outside Ecruteak City thinking a small, local tournament would be an easy thing for him to win. After all, he had plenty of experience from the Indigo and Orange Leagues. After breezing through the first few battles, Ash faced Ephraim's Skiploom in the final. Despite Ash and Bulbasaur having more experience in battle, they had no answer to Skiploom's adaptability, as it unleashed an unexpected Solar Beam mid-battle.

TRAINER TALES

IN THE JOHTO REGION

A new region means a whole new world of possibilities and adventures for Ash and his friends. These are some of the notable moments from Ash's journey through the Johto region.

1 LEGENDARY SIGHTING!

When they first arrived, Ash, Misty and Brock got lost in the foggy woods. They came to a lake, where they spotted a mysterious, shimmering figure standing on a small island. The three friends looked in awe at the creature, which turned towards them, jumped to the far side of the lake and faded into thin air. The Pokémon they saw on the lake was the Legendary Suicune. It was a good omen for Ash's time in the Johto region.

2 ANCIENT LEGENDS OF THE JOHTO REGION

While in the Burned Tower in Ecruteak City, Ash learned about Ho-Oh, the Legendary bird Pokémon, guardian of the skies, who he saw when he first left Pallet Town with Pikachu. Ho-Oh was believed to have vanished from the world three centuries before. Sightings were rare and said to be reserved for only the greatest Pokémon Trainers. The Burned Tower, formally the Bell Tower, was the only place that Ho-Oh would appear to its chosen humans. Until one day, intruders stormed the tower, wanting to use Ho-Oh's powers for evil, and it fled, never contacting humans again.

3 INTERRUPTED DELIVERY

When Ash was cleaning his Poké Balls beside a stream, a Quagsire jumped out of the water and stole the GS Ball that he was supposed to be delivering to Professor Oak! Every year, the Quagsire steal objects from Cherrygrove City for their annual celebration at Blue Moon Falls, where they use Water Gun to shoot the objects over the falls. The local people go to the river after the ritual and retrieve their objects, believing they will now bring them good luck. After defeating Team Rocket, and watching the Quagsire complete their ritual, Ash got his GS Ball back. He was not looking forward to explaining it to the professor!

4 ASH GOES ON A MOUNTAIN MISSION

Ash is always willing to help a friend in need, so when he ran into Todd Snap he decided to join him on his adventure. Todd wanted to take a picture of the Legendary bird, Articuno, who was rumoured to help lost travellers high up on the mountain. Just at the moment they spotted Articuno, Team Rocket appeared – right on cue! They had plans to capture the Pokémon for Giovanni. The battle with Team Rocket knocked Ash, Todd and Pikachu into a ravine. The powerful Articuno took out Team Rocket easily and they were blasted off … again! Articuno then sent an Ice Beam through some rocks to make a path so that Ash, Todd and Pikachu could be rescued. Todd was able to take a fantastic photo of the Legendary Pokémon. Todd then decided to stay up in the mountains in the hope of getting more pictures.

5 SNORLAX THE SUMO CHAMP

Ash was the first rookie to reach the final of the Pokémon Sumo Competition with his Snorlax. They were up against Raiden and his Feraligatr, the reigning champions. This was purely a wrestling competition – Pokémon were banned from using any special attacks. Even though Feraligatr was the stronger competitor, Snorlax was deceptively agile and managed to take the victory. The reward was one year's supply of food, which Snorlax managed to finish immediately.

6 CHIKORITA TO THE RESCUE

While out looking for firewood, Ash and his Chikorita found themselves accidentally trapped in a building owned by the electric company. It was protected by Electric-type Pokémon and Ash had to fight his way out. Team Rocket had also entered the building, and while Chikorita was battling an Electabuzz, the dastardly trio locked the two Pokémon in a cage. Ash chased after Team Rocket, who used Arbok and Victreebell to attack him. Chikorita tried its best to break out of the cage to help Ash, but it wasn't strong enough. Suddenly, it evolved into the powerful Bayleef! Ash and Bayleef became an unstoppable team, defeating Team Rocket and the Electabuzz.

7 BULBASAUR THE PEACEKEEPER

When Ash called Professor Oak, he found out that a three-way turf war had erupted on the Oak Corral. The Grass types, Water types and a visiting troop of Hoppip, Skiploom and Jumpluff were fighting over territory. Oak asked Ash to send in his Bulbasaur to help, as he knew it had experience looking after all the Pokémon in the Hidden Village. Bulbasaur used Solar Beam and stopped everyone from fighting, and they all came together in a peace dance. There was still some tension, so Oak asked if he could keep Bulbasaur as a peacekeeper for a little while longer. Ash proudly agreed.

8 THE RED GYARADOS OF LAKE RAGE

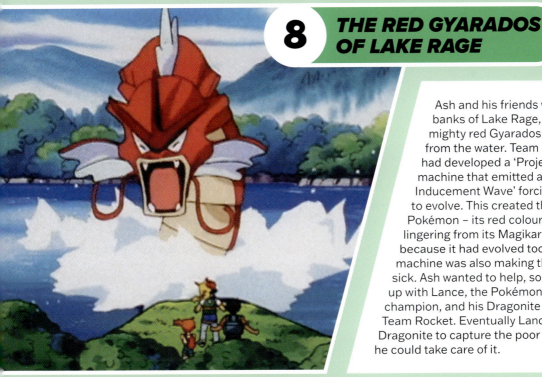

Ash and his friends were on the banks of Lake Rage, where a mighty red Gyarados appeared from the water. Team Rocket had developed a 'Project R' machine that emitted an 'Evolution Inducement Wave' forcing Pokémon to evolve. This created the unusual Pokémon – its red colour was lingering from its Magikarp stage because it had evolved too quickly. The machine was also making the Pokémon sick. Ash wanted to help, so he teamed up with Lance, the Pokémon League champion, and his Dragonite to stop Team Rocket. Eventually Lance used his Dragonite to capture the poor Gyarados so he could take care of it.

BATTLE BREAKDOWN

THE JOHTO REGION GYM

VIOLET CITY GYM

ZEPHYR BADGE

Faulkner, the Violet City Gym Leader, always wanted to fly as a boy, and is passionate about Flying-type Pokémon. He surprises Ash by arriving for the battle on a hang-glider.

BATTLE 1

 v

HOOTHOOT* — CHIKORITA

BATTLE 2

 v

HOOTHOOT — PIKACHU*

AZALEA TOWN GYM

HIVE BADGE

It looked like this would be a tricky battle for Ash without Charizard, but he still had his Cyndaquil – would it be strong enough? The gym leader is a specialist in Bug-type Pokémon.

BATTLE 1

 v

SPINARAK* — CYNDAQUIL

BATTLE 2

 v

SPINARAK — CHIKORITA*

GOLDENROD CITY GYM

PLAIN BADGE

Ash had already battled Whitney and lost, but after visiting Whitney's farm, Ash figured out teamwork was the best strategy to overcome her Miltank's powerful Rollout move.

BATTLE 1

 v

MILTANK* — CYNDAQUIL

ECRUTEAK CITY GYM

FOG BADGE

With a strategy in place, thanks to Nurse Joy, Ash was ready to face Morty's powerful Gengar. This was a 3-on-3 battle where the gym leader was not allowed to make substitutions.

BATTLE 1

 v

GASTLY* — NOCTOWL

BATTLE 2

 v

GASTLY* — PIKACHU

After registering to enter the Johto League, Ash travelled to challenge the gym leaders in the Johto region. He needed to earn eight badges in order to compete in the Johto Silver League.

* winner
** winner after a match forfeit
*** interrupted battle

BATTLE 3

 V

DODRIO | PIKACHU*

BATTLE 4

 V

PIDGEOT* | PIKACHU

BATTLE 5

 V

PIDGEOT | CHARIZARD*

Despite Faulkner's confidence in his undefeatable Flying types, Pidgeot is no match for Ash's Charizard, who wins with a Seismic Toss.

BATTLE 3

 V

METAPOD* | CHIKORITA

BATTLE 4

 V

METAPOD | PIKACHU*

BATTLE 5

 V

SCYTHER* | PIKACHU

BATTLE 6

 V

SCYTHER | CYNDAQUIL*

BATTLE 2

 V

MILTANK* | TOTODILE

BATTLE 3

 V

MILTANK | PIKACHU*

Pikachu lands a Thunderbolt to win!

BATTLE 3

 V

GASTLY | CYNDAQUIL*

BATTLE 4

 V

HAUNTER* | CYNDAQUIL

BATTLE 5

 V

HAUNTER | NOCTOWL*

BATTLE 6

GENGAR | NOCTOWL*

CIANWOOD CITY GYM

STORM BADGE

After Ash saw the gym leader, Chuck, sparring with his Machoke on the beach, he knew he was in for an intense battle. However, Chuck was tired out and bruised from his practice session, giving Ash the advantage.

BATTLE 1

POLIWRATH*

V

PIKACHU

OLIVINE CITY GYM

MINERAL BADGE

It's finally time to battle Jasmine for the Mineral Badge. Ash had seen Jasmine's Steelix in battle against Team Rocket, so he knew he was in for a great match. Jasmine promised not to go easy on Ash and came out swinging.

BATTLE 1

MAGNEMITE

V

PIKACHU*

MAHOGANY TOWN GYM

GLACIER BADGE

After Ash helped him find his beloved Piloswine, Pryce remembered that Trainers and Pokémon could be friends. In the last battle, Pryce forfeited the match to keep his favourite Pokémon safe.

BATTLE 1

DEWGONG

V

CYNDAQUIL*

BLACKTHORN CITY GYM

RISING BADGE

Team Rocket had caused all kinds of chaos by stealing an ancient relic and angering a Dragonite. Ash and his friends had to help Blackthorn City Gym Leader, Clair, restore peace to her gym before the battle could commence.

BATTLE 1

KINGDRA

V

SNORLAX*

BATTLE 2

GYARADOS*

V

SNORLAX

BATTLE 2

 V

POLIWRATH — **BAYLEEF***

BATTLE 3

 V

MACHOKE — **BAYLEEF***

Machoke was relentless with its Karate Chops, but Bayleef's Vine Whip and Razor Leaf takes it down.

BATTLE 2

 V

STEELIX* — **PIKACHU**

BATTLE 3

 V

STEELIX — **CYNDAQUIL***

Steelix's Sandstorm came under fire from Cyndaquil.

BATTLE 2

 V

PILOSWINE* — **CYNDAQUIL**

BATTLE 3

 V

PILOSWINE — **PIKACHU****

Piloswine's Blizzard attack covers the battlefield in snow and forms giant ice pillars. Cool!

BATTLE 3

 V

GYARADOS — **PIKACHU***

BATTLE 4

 V

DRAGONAIR* — **PIKACHU**

BATTLE 5

 V

DRAGONAIR — **CHARIZARD***

THE WHIRL CUP

The Whirl Cup takes place on the Whirl Islands, located in the sea between the cities of Cianwood and Olivine in the Johto region. It is a competition for Water-type Pokémon, which happens every three years. It takes place over six days and the winner is crowned as Water Pokémon Alpha Omega.

* winner
** winner after a match forfeit
*** interrupted battle

ROUND 1 Ash v Christopher

Ash takes on an experienced Water-type Trainer.

BATTLE 1

TOTODILE* V KINGDRA

This was a tricky match-up for Totodile given Kingdra's dual Water and Dragon type. Ash had Totodile hide in the water and jump out at close range. Totodile used Bite on Kingdra's snout just as it did Hydro Pump. Kingdra swelled up full of water and blasted across the field.

Misty v Harrison

Misty is up against a very arrogant opponent.

BATTLE 2

CORSOLA* V QWILFISH

This battle was closely fought between the two Pokémon, with both using some powerful moves. When Qwilfish jumped out of the water, it had Corsola stuck in its crown of horns. Misty used the advantage and fired a close-range Spike Cannon, which knocked out Qwilfish.

ROUND 2 Misty v Ash

Ash usually beats Misty, but water is her speciality.

BATTLE 1

POLIWHIRL* V TOTODILE

After the first exchange of attacks, Totodile was left dazed, but still managed to duck Poliwhirl's Double Slap attack. After a Headbutt from Totodile and some athletic jumps from Poliwhirl, Ash ordered a Water Gun, but Poliwhirl dodged it and did Double Slap to win.

BATTLE 2

POLIWHIRL V KINGLER*

Kingler blocked Poliwhirl's Bubble move with its claw before unleashing a Crabhammer. The attack struck the water, which caused whirlpools to form in the arena. The energy knocked Poliwhirl into the whirlpools, allowing Kingler to knock it out.

BATTLE 3

PSYDUCK* V KINGLER

Misty tried to call Corsola but out came Psyduck instead! It immediately fell into the water, nearly drowning itself. Psyduck seemed completely outmatched, until Misty had it use Confusion, which launched Kingler backwards. Misty claimed her first victory against Ash.

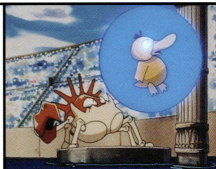

ROUND 3 Misty v Trinity

POLIWHIRL AND CORSOLA V GYARADOS AND CHINCHOU*

After knocking Ash out in the previous round, Misty was defeated by Trinity, who eventually came second in the Whirl Cup tournament.

JOHTO SILVER LEAGUE

To enter the Johto Silver League, a Trainer must first earn eight Johto Gym badges. There are four stages of the Silver League: Athlete Screening Rounds, Round Robin semi-finals, Victory Tournament and then the final.

* win
**win by withdrawal of opponent
***double knockout

ATHLETE SCREENING ROUNDS

Designed to trim down the field of 200 Trainers to 48. These are a series of 1-on-1 battles, with no Trainer having to battle more than three times. Ash won all three of his battles.

ROUND ROBIN SEMI-FINALS

The 48 Trainers who made it through the Screening Rounds are then sorted into groups of three. Each faced the other in a series of 3-on-3 battles. The Trainer from each group with the most points advanced to the Victory Tournament.

VICTORY TOURNAMENT

It all builds up to this! 16 Trainers. 6-on-6 battles in a packed stadium. The battlefield can rotate between types (Grass, Rock, Water and Ice) and a computer randomly selects the battlefield at the beginning of each match.

ROUND 1 Gary v Ash

BATTLEFIELD TYPE: Rock

BATTLE 1 — NIDOQUEEN* V TAUROS

Gary ordered Nidoqueen to grab Tauros by the horns and it launched a close-range Hyper Beam, which knocked Tauros out.

BATTLE 2 — MAGMAR V HERACROSS*

Magmar used a Flamethrower, but Heracross blew the fire away with its wings. Heracross knocked out Magmar with Megahorn.

BATTLE 3 — BLASTOISE* V HERACROSS

Heracross hid behind a rock, but Blastoise's Hydro Pump managed to blast through the rock and knocked Heracross out.

BATTLE 4 — BLASTOISE* V MUK
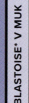

Muk absorbed Blastoise and tried to smother it, but Blastoise used Hydro Pump to blast out of Muk, so Ash recalled it.

BATTLE 5

BLASTOISE* V BAYLEEF

Bayleef avoided a Hydro Pump attack with a Vine Whip-powered jump. Both Pokémon exchanged blows, but Blastoise was the victor.

BATTLE 6

ARCANINE V SNORLAX*

Snorlax was able to free itself from Arcanine's Fire Spin attack. It then landed a direct hit with Hyper Beam, causing Arcanine to faint.

BATTLE 7

NIDOQUEEN V SNORLAX*

Nidoqueen opened by using its tail to jump into the air. Nidoqueen then tried Hyper Beam, but Snorlax returned with Ice Punch to win.

BATTLE 8

SCIZOR* V SNORLAX

Snorlax started the battle with a Hyper Beam, but the quick Scizor hit back with a powerful Metal Claw and knocked Snorlax out.

BATTLE 9

SCIZOR* V MUK

Muk absorbed Scizor's Metal Claw but Scizor used the moment to throw its opponent into the air. It then used Swift to defeat Muk for the win.

BATTLE 10

SCIZOR V CHARIZARD*

Scizor attacked with Steel Wing, and Charizard responded with Flamethrower. Scizor tried to evade the attack, but Charizard won.

BATTLE 11

GOLEM V CHARIZARD*

Charizard tried to use Seismic Toss, but Golem was too heavy. Golem then tried to use Rollout, but Charizard used Dragon Rage and knocked it out.

BATTLE 12

BLASTOISE* V CHARIZARD

Ash and Gary were both down to their last Pokémon. Charizard burned the field, then Blastoise tried to put it out with Hydro Pump, which just created lots of steam. When the steam cleared, Blastoise and Charizard were locked in close-range combat, until Charizard used a Seismic Toss. Blastoise was slammed into the ground and didn't get back up.

ROUND 2 Harrison v Ash

BATTLEFIELD TYPE: Grass

BATTLE 1

KECLEON V PIKACHU*

Pikachu hid in the long grass, but Kecleon mowed it down using its tongue. Pikachu grabbed Kecleon's tongue and used it as a wire to deliver a Thunderbolt.

BATTLE 2

SNEASEL* V PIKACHU

Pikachu used Thunderbolt, but Harrison's recently caught Sneasel dodged it. The stubborn Pokémon attacked Pikachu with Metal Claw to win the round.

BATTLE 3

SNEASEL V TOTODILE*

Totodile used Water Gun, then Bite on Sneasel's arm, immobilising it. Totodile ended the battle by doing a happy dance, finally knocking out Sneasel with its tail.

BATTLE 4

HYPNO* V TOTODILE

Totodile began with Scary Face, but Hypno was unphased. It used Hypnosis to take control of Totodile, and sent Totodile flying off the field with Psychic.

BATTLE 5

HYPNO V SNORLAX*

Snorlax was asleep when it came out of its Poké Ball, so Hypno used Dream Eater. Snorlax woke up in a rage and used a single Hyper Beam attack to defeat Hypno.

BATTLE 6
STEELIX V NOCTOWL

Noctowl attempted Hypnosis but was outmatched. Its ability to fly made it easy prey for Steelix's powerful Iron Tail, which knocked Noctowl out of the sky.

BATTLE 7
STEELIX V SNORLAX*

Steelix used Bind and Crunch against Snorlax, but the Normal type freed itself using Ice Punch. Snorlax finished Steelix off with a mighty Hyper Beam attack.

BATTLE 8
HOUNDOOM* V SNORLAX

Houndoom used Counter against Snorlax's final Hyper Beam, blasting it with its own move at twice its original power. Snorlax was knocked out.

BATTLE 9
HOUNDOOM V BAYLEEF*

Bayleef used Vine Whip to shut Houndoom's muzzle and prevent further attacks, then tossed it to the ground before using Body Slam to win the battle.

BATTLE 10
BLAZIKEN* V BAYLEEF

Bayleef's vines were easily caught by Blaziken. Ash ordered a Body Slam but Blaziken landed a close-range Fire Punch and knocked Bayleef out.

BATTLE 11
BLAZIKEN* V CHARIZARD

Blaziken and Charizard both started off with Flamethrowers, which collided to form a giant cloud of smoke. The pair exchanged attacks, but just managed to tire each other out. As the smoke cleared, Charizard was so exhausted that it fainted.

WELCOME TO THE ...
HOENN REGION

The environment varies dramatically across the Hoenn region, from rainforests to deserts. It is covered in forests, mountains and waterways, and surrounded by 16 coastal cities. The citizens of the Hoenn region enjoy a much warmer climate than neighbouring regions.

Towering above the centre of the Hoenn region is Mt. Chimney, an active volcano that is always smoking. The landscape surrounding the volcano features delightful hot springs.

BADGES ASH WON

In the Hoenn region, Pokémon Trainers must earn eight badges from Hoenn gym leaders before they can enter the annual Hoenn League Championship in Ever Grande City.

Gym Leader:
Roxanne
Rustboro City Gym
Type: Rock

STONE

Gym Leader:
Brawly
Dewford Island Gym
Type: Fighting

KNUCKLE

Gym Leader:
Wattson
Mauville City Gym
Type: Electric

DYNAMO

Gym Leader:
Flannery
Lavaridge Town Gym
Type: Fire

HEAT

Gym Leader:
Norman
Petalburg City Gym
Type: Normal

BALANCE

Gym Leader:
Winona
Fortree City Gym
Type: Flying

FEATHER

Gym Leader:
Tate and Liza
Mossdeep City Gym
Type: Psychic

MIND

Gym Leader:
Juan
Sootopolis City Gym
Type: Water

RAIN

COMPETITIONS

The thrill of competition follows Ash to the Hoenn region! When he arrives in Crossgate Town he takes part in the PokéRinger, where a Trainer and a Flying-type Pokémon compete to grab a ring and land it on a goalpost.

THE CROSSGATE POKÉRINGER – WINNER
Ash entered with his Taillow. First, they had to retrieve a ring from a hot-air balloon, and hang the ring on a goalpost. The final was Ash versus James, from Team Rocket, and his Dustox. James did PokéRinger training as a child. A flash tornado appeared, and Ash sent Taillow into it, causing it to spin out. Taillow evolved into Swellow and used Wing Attack to grab the ring. Dustox knocked the ring out of Swellow's beak and they both dived for it. Swellow knocked the ring on to the goalpost.

ASH'S CATCHES

Before travelling to the Hoenn region, Ash left his Pokémon at Oak's Corral (except Pikachu) so he could learn all about the new Pokémon.

TAILLOW / SWELLOW

TYPE:
Normal/Flying

Taillow was the first Pokémon that Ash caught in the Hoenn region! Swellow is tough and persistent. It is stubborn and will fight on rather than give up. In the gym battle at Sootopolis, Swellow slammed Juan's Wiscash and defeated Spenser's Venusaur using Aerial Ace.

TREECKO / GROVYLE / SCEPTILE

TYPE:
Grass

Treecko is cool, calm and extremely loyal to those it cares about. Sceptile is undeniably powerful – along with Pikachu, it has battled the most Legendaries including Tobias's Darkrai and Latios, Brandon's Regirock, and Deoxys in the Battle Frontier.

CORPHISH

TYPE:
Water

Corphish is very brash, finds it hard to make friends, and it will often charge into things without thinking first. Corphish is also incredibly strong, but Ash struggled to teach Corphish to handle its own strength. Ash used it against Tyson's Hariyama, Swampert and Arcanine.

TORKOAL

TYPE:
Fire

Torkoal is very emotional and particularly friendly to all people and Pokémon. It will often cry when it is happy, which releases smoke from its nostrils. It conclusively won against Tyson's Shifty during the Hoenn League Championship. It also bravely faced Tobias's Mythical Darkrai.

SNORUNT / GLALIE

TYPE:
Ice

As a Snorunt, it is mischievous and troublesome. It seems to laugh at everything – whether good or bad! It often freezes Ash as a sign of affection. During the Ever Grande Conference, Glalie was a powerhouse, defeating Clark's Charizard and Morrison's Metang.

PROFESSOR BIRCH

Professor Birch is the region professor for the Hoenn region. His lab is in Littleroot Town, but you won't find him there very often because he 'doesn't want to stay cooped up in his lab'.

Professor Birch prefers to be out and about, studying Pokémon's habits and behaviours where they live – in forests, on top of mountains or in water. This means he often runs into Ash and his friends when they are out on their adventures.

One of his favourite subjects to study is strange Evolutions. When Ash and his friends ran into him on Island A of the tropical A-B-C Islands, he explained that a Deep Sea Tooth caused Clamperl to evolve into a Huntail, and that a Deep Sea Scale was needed to obtain a Gorebyss. He was further exploring the mystery around these two Evolution methods.

As region professor, he gifts new Trainers with their first Pokémon. The first partners here are Torchic, Treecko and Mudkip.

MAY

May's first love is travel and adventure. She never intended to become a Pokémon Trainer, and has proven herself to be a hard-working and talented Pokémon coordinator.

May is a sweet and optimistic girl. As the daughter of Norman, Petalburg City's gym leader, she was expected to follow in his footsteps and become a Pokémon Trainer too, but she wasn't keen on the idea. May had a dislike of Pokémon that started as a child when she was swarmed by Tentacool. Eventually, after meeting Ash and another coordinator, Janet, May started to show interest in Pokémon contests and gradually became a great coordinator. May has formed a strong bond with her first two Pokémon, Torchic and Wurmple.

WHEN MAY MET ASH

May went to meet Professor Birch to get her first Pokémon, but he wasn't in the lab, he was in the woods helping Ash and Pikachu. After Team Rocket captured Pikachu, it unleashed a huge electric attack which fried May's bike to a crisp. Shocking!

MAX

Max dreams of being a great Trainer one day. Despite not having any Pokémon of his own, he has formed close bonds with several already, including the Legendary Deoxys.

Max is May's younger brother. He is fascinated by Pokémon and wants to learn everything he can about them. He is passionate and  dedicated to becoming a Pokémon Trainer one day, just like his father. Their parents want Max to travel with May and Ash so that he can learn about Pokémon in real life rather than from books.

HOW MAX MET ASH

Ash challenged Norman, Max's father, to a gym battle. It was the first time Max saw his father lose in battle and he was very upset, but his father explained that losing is an important part of being a gym leader.

TEAM MAGMA

Tech-loving Team Magma are a force of nature and their ultimate goal is to take over the world using their sophisticated machinery and a sneaky plan to capture a Legendary Pokémon ...

TEAM MAGMA'S LEADER: MAXIE

Their plan for taking over the world depended on making more ground – literally – with magma! They believed that with more territory, humanity would have more space to build, develop and live. To help them achieve this, the plan was to capture the Legendary Pokémon, Groudon, and the Orb that controls it. They had a lot of tech to help them with their mission: a meteorite-powered laser, a boat and a submarine.

GROUDON

TEAM MAGMA v TEAM AQUA

In their quest for the Legendary Pokémon, Team Magma ended up catching Kyogre, while Team Aqua had secretly caught Groudon. When the power of the Orbs that control the Legendary Pokémon was accidentally absorbed by Pikachu and Archie, Kyogre and Groudon almost wrecked an entire island with an explosive battle. With some help from Ash, his friends, Lance and, inadvertently, Team Rocket, peace was finally restored and a new island was created.

TEAM AQUA

Water-wielding Team Aqua have plans for ocean-based world domination. This untrustworthy team will stop at nothing in their attempts to catch the Legendary Pokémon, Kyogre ...

TEAM AQUA'S LEADER: ARCHIE

KYOGRE

Like Team Magma, Team Aqua have their own ideas for world domination. Their plans, though, involve the ocean as they want to gain enough power to see the sea dominate the whole world. One of their plans was to capture and control the Legendary Pokémon, Kyogre, which ended in disaster. Team Aqua travel around the region by submarine or jetpack. Much like their fiery rivals, their plans very rarely succeed.

TRAINER TIPS

THE HOENN REGION

LEARN NEW MOVES TOGETHER

Before his gym battle in Rustboro Gym, Ash and Pikachu were trying to learn something new – Iron Tail, a Steel-type move. This was the first one Ash taught any of his Pokémon, rather than them learning it naturally. Learning this move took a lot of time and effort for both Ash and Pikachu, mainly because Pikachu had to strengthen and fully develop its tail first. Pikachu went into the Rustboro Gym battle without having fully mastered the move, and it failed a few times during the match. But perseverance pulled them through, and Pikachu performed Iron Tail perfectly for the first time. The determined duo won the Stone Badge.

TRY TO KEEP CALM

Ash had a reasonable amount of success up to this point, and his confidence had grown – perhaps too much. For his first gym battle with Brawley, Ash went in with power and strength, rather than strategy. Towards the end of the battle, this power-only tactic stopped working. Midway through the battle, Makuhita evolved into the powerful Hariyama, and Treecko was tired. Both Brock and Brawley told Ash that Treecko had reached its limit, but Ash did not listen – he wanted to win. After their defeat, Ash felt guilty for putting winning above his Pokémon's health and safety. Brawley told him that if he'd just had a level head, kept calm and strategised, he would probably have won. This was a piece of advice Ash took to heart and worked on throughout the rest of his journey in the Hoenn region.

After speaking with Gary, Ash realised that what he needed to do was to start again and seek out a challenge, an adventure in a unexplored land where he could learn about all new Pokémon. Here are some of the lessons Ash picked up on his journey from the Hoenn region.

STRATEGISE!

When Ash ran into Corphish and he saw how powerful, quick and strong it was, he knew he had to catch it. In the battle to catch Corphish, Ash started to put Brawley's words of wisdom into practice. After Pikachu failed to land an attack on Corphish, Ash changed strategy. He brought out Treecko, so Corphish's water moves wouldn't have an effect. Ash told Treecko to use Focus and then wait, using Corphish's impatience and territorial nature against it and eventually succeeded.

BUILD A STRONG TEAM

Ash built his team from scratch when he started his adventure in the Hoenn region. He had learned enough to know not to just include Pokémon with the strongest and most powerful moves, but a well-rounded team that left him room for strategy. Ash was able to use the unique strengths of his new Pokémon to their advantage, and this helped him to really step up his skill in battle.

GLALIE

GROVYLE

TORKOAL

SWELLOW

CORPHISH

PIKACHU

TRAINER TALES

It's a fresh start for Ash, with a whole new Pokémon team and some new travel companions too! Here are some cool moments from Ash's time in the Hoenn region.

1 FIRST POKÉMON CAUGHT

The PokéDex for Taillow states they are fierce and don't back down, and this was especially true for Ash's Taillow! When they first met, Taillow battled against Ash's Pikachu, and it managed to burst out of a Thunderbolt attack. Luckily May, Max, Brock and his Forretress turned up to save Ash and Pikachu at the last moment. Later, Taillow returned to Ash, wanting to battle Pikachu again, to finally prove who was best. Pikachu and Taillow had a fast-paced battle and were equally matched; both quick, powerful and relentless. Ash caught Taillow before it could damage itself any more. Taillow was Ash's first Hoenn region Pokémon.

2 POKÉMON CONTESTS

When May found out about Pokémon contests, she decided she wanted to be a contest coordinator. She had developed a love and appreciation for Pokémon, but was not interested in traditional battling. Instead, she was enamoured by the beauty and joy of Pokémon and how they move – contests were her true calling! Travelling with Ash taught her many things, and gave her the courage and confidence to follow her dreams. After overcoming a few defeats, May finally won her first contest ribbon with Beautifly.

3 'MY DAD IS MY HERO!'

Watching his dad, Norman, battle his friend, Ash, was difficult for Max to watch. And it only got harder for him when Ash beat his dad … how could his hero lose like this? Confused and angry, Max stole Ash's Balance Badge and ran away. At first, no one knew where he had gone, but luckily they found him hiding in the greenhouse. Norman explained to Max how important losing was because it teaches you so much. Ash said that Max could keep the badge if he wanted, as battling his dad had already made him a lot better and stronger, and with that Max came out of the greenhouse and gave Ash his badge back. All was forgiven!

4 A NEW USE FOR PELIPPER'S BEAK!

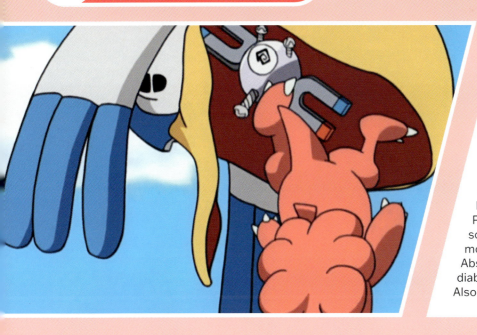

There are lots of uses for a Pelipper's huge beak, though it is mainly used to deliver packages and letters all around the region. But as Ash discovered while on route to Rustboro, a Pelipper's beak can also be used to hide other Pokémon in during battle, so it can do out-of-type moves! Was this cheating? Absolutely. But was it a diabolically genius plan? Also yes!

5 NEW BATTLE TYPES

In the Hoenn region, Ash learned about Double Battles, which is when two Pokémon fight against two opponents. Sometimes the two Pokémon are from one Trainer, or sometimes two Trainers team up and send one Pokémon each into battle. The battle continues until both Pokémon from one side can't continue. Ash's first Double Battle was against Forrester Franklin, who sent Aridos and Yanma while Ash used Pikachu and Treecko. It was a great display of Ash's growth as a Trainer as he adapted to a new situation, learned new rules and made a fantastic team out of his oldest Pokémon, Pikachu, and newest one, Treecko.

6 SAVING AN ELECTRIC-TYPE REFUGE

After taking Pikachu to the Pokémon Centre for treatment, Ash found out his Pokémon pal was supercharged during the gym battle and it had been an unfair win. Ash headed to the Power Plant to give Wattson back his badge. That's where they all ran into Team Rocket! The Trio wanted to use the plant as a base for their operations in the Hoenn region. But before they could do that they needed to clear it of all the Voltorbs and Magnemites who had taken up refuge there. As a bonus, they knew they could present all these new Pokémon to their boss, Giovanni. Wattson and Ash fought together to protect the Pokémon and the plant, and Pikachu ended up blasting Team Rocket away with a huge Thunderbolt. Wattson was very grateful for Ash's help in protecting the plant and the two agreed to have a rematch in the future.

PIKACHU AMNESIA

There was a time when Team Rocket were successful in getting Pikachu to join their team … and all it took was Pikachu getting amnesia! Meowth took advantage of Pikachu's memory loss and told it that it had always been part of Team Rocket. During their time together, Meowth saw how brave and kind Pikachu was. Eventually Pikachu got its memory back and affectionately licked Ash's face to show it remembered him again!

8

BATTLING FRIENDS

When Ash met Morrison, they became friends immediately; they both loved battling and were just as competitive as each other! When they were matched up to face each other in the Victory Tournament, Morrison found the idea of battling his friend difficult to come to terms with. Morrison didn't put any effort into the match when they came face to face. Finally, Ash persuaded him that real friends made sure they battled to the best of their ability. Morrison understood, and after this moment, the two friends had an epic battle.

BATTLE BREAKDOWN

THE HOENN REGION GYM

RUSTBORO CITY GYM

STONE BADGE

ROXANNE V ASH
Pikachu had recently learned Iron Tail, giving it a surprise attack not true to its type. This battle was 2-on-2.

BATTLE 1

GEODUDE*

V

TREECKO

DEWFORD ISLAND GYM

KNUCKLE BADGE

BRAWLY V ASH
Ash told Pikachu to sit this match out as he had a new strategy to try. This battle was 2-on-2, with only the challenger being able to use a substitute.

BATTLE 1

MACHOP

V

TREECKO**

MAUVILLE CITY GYM

DYNAMO BADGE

WATTSON V ASH
Wattson surprised Ash by revealing the three Pokémon he'd be using at the start of the match. It was a 3-on-3 battle.

BATTLE 1

MAGNEMITE

V

PIKACHU*

LAVARIDGE TOWN GYM

HEAT BADGE

FLANNERY V ASH
Flannery had only taken over the gym from her grandfather three days before facing Ash. This was a 3-on-3 battle.

BATTLE 1

BATTLE 2

MAGCARGO

V

CORPHISH*

SLUGMA**

V

TREECKO

Ash needed eight badges from Hoenn League gyms before he could enter the League Championship. To challenge himself in this new region, Ash left all his Pokémon in Oak's Corral, so he could truly start again and learn about the region's Pokémon for himself.

* winner
** winner after a match withdrawal
*** interrupted battle
**** double KO
***** faints

BATTLE 2

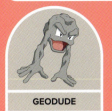 **V**

GEODUDE | PIKACHU*

BATTLE 3

 **V**

NOSEPASS | PIKACHU*

Pikachu won Ash his first Hoenn League badge.

BATTLE 2

 **V**

MACHOP | CORPHISH*

BATTLE 3

 **V**

HARIYAMA* | CORPHISH

BATTLE 4

 V

HARIYAMA | TREECKO*

BATTLE 2

 **V**

VOLTORB | PIKACHU*

BATTLE 3

 V

MAGNETON | PIKACHU*

BATTLE 3

 V

SLUGMA** | CORPHISH

BATTLE 4

 V

SLUGMA | PIKACHU*

BATTLE 5

 V

TORKOAL* | PIKACHU

BATTLE 6

 V

TORKOAL | CORPHISH*

PETALBURG CITY GYM

BALANCE BADGE

NORMAN V ASH

Norman and Ash had an unofficial 1-on-1 battle when they first met, with Norman's Vigoroth defeating Pikachu. This was a 3-on-3 battle, with only Ash being allowed to make substitutions.

BATTLE 1

 V

SLAKOTH** | PIKACHU

BATTLE 2

 V

SLAKOTH | TORKOAL*

FORTREE CITY GYM

FEATHER BADGE

WINONA V ASH

This gym battle took place on elevated platforms, high up in the air. This was a 3-on-3 battle, with only the challenger being allowed to make substitutions.

BATTLE 1

ALTARIA | GROVYLE*

BATTLE 2

 V

PELIPPER**** | PIKACHU****

MOSSDEEP CITY GYM

MIND BADGE

TATE AND LIZA V ASH

This Double Battle was on an unusual battlefield, with a mock-up of the planets floating in mid-air, which could be used as obstacles. The winner needed to knock out both Pokémon from the opposing team.

BATTLE

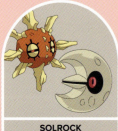 V

SOLROCK AND LUNATONE | PIKACHU AND SWELLOW*

SOOTOPOLIS CITY GYM

RAIN BADGE

JUAN V ASH

The Sootopolis Gym had a complicated set-up! Each participant used five Pokémon, with the first round being a Double Battle, and the second round was single battles.

BATTLE 1

 V

SEALEO AND SEAKING | PIKACHU AND SNORUT*****

BATTLE 2

 V

SEALEO AND SEAKING | PIKACHU AND CORPHISH*

BATTLE 3

 V

VIGOROTH*   TORKOAL

BATTLE 4

 V

VIGOROTH****   PIKACHU****

BATTLE 5

 V

SLAKING   GROVYLE*

BATTLE 3

 V

SWELLOW*   GROVYLE

BATTLE 4

SWELLOW   SWELLOW*

BATTLE 3

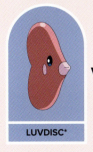 V

LUVDISC*   GROVYLE

BATTLE 4

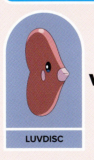 V

LUVDISC   CORPHISH*

BATTLE 5

 V

WHISCASH*   CORPHISH

BATTLE 6

 V

WHISCASH   SWELLOW*

BATTLE 7

 V

MILOTIC*   SWELLOW

BATTLE 8

 V

MILOTIC   PIKACHU*

HOENN LEAGUE CHAMPIONSHIP

The Hoenn League Championship happens in Ever Grande City every year. Each entrant must earn eight gym badges to compete. The stadium facilities are amazing, the central large stadium is an island in a lake and is surrounded by smaller battle stadiums.

* winner
** winner after a match withdrawal
*** interrupted battle
**** double KO
***** faints

PRELIMINARY ROUNDS
These rounds trim the competitors down from 600 to 256 with 1-on-1 battles, where entrants must register the Pokémon they plan to use before they battle.

QUALIFYING TOURNAMENT
For this stage, the Trainers must win all three Double Battle rounds to be one of the 32 competitors who advance to participate in the Victory Tournament.

VICTORY TOURNAMENT
This stage of knock-out rounds happens in the main stadium. These are full 6-on-6 battles on a battlefield that rotates between Grass, Rock, Water and Ice. The victor needs to win all of their final rounds, meaning they must defeat five opponents in a row.

ROUND 1 Katie v Ash*

BATTLEFIELD TYPE: Rock

BATTLE 1 VENOMOTH V TORKOAL**

BATTLE 2 GOLDUCK* V TORKOAL

BATTLE 3 DUGTRIO* V PIKACHU

BATTLE 4 DUGTRIO V GLALIE*

BATTLE 5 MISDREAVUS***** V GLALIE****

BATTLE 6 GOLDUCK V CORPHISH*

BATTLE 7 VENOMOTH** V CORPHISH

BATTLE 8
VENOMOTH V
SWELLOW*

BATTLE 9
SCIZOR V
SWELLOW*

BATTLE 10
WALREIN* V
SWELLOW

BATTLE 11
WALREIN V
CORPHISH

BATTLE 12
WALREIN V
GROVYLE*

Walrein started the final match-up with Ice Beam, which Grovyle dodged. Grovyle used Leaf Blade on the water, which caused a shock wave that blasted Walrein. Katie ordered Walrein to use its Mimicked Quick Attack. At the last moment, Ash ordered Grovyle to use another Leaf Blade. This sent Walrein up to the sky, and when it landed, it was knocked out.

ROUND 2 Morrison v Ash*

BATTLEFIELD TYPE: Ice / Grass

BATTLE 1
GIRAFARIG V
CORPHISH*

BATTLE 2
GROWLITHE V
CORPHISH*

BATTLE 3
SWAMPERT**** V
CORPHISH****

BATTLE 4
STEELIX* V
PIKACHU

BATTLE 5
STEELIX* V
TORKOAL

BATTLE 6
STEELIX V
GROVYLE*

BATTLE 7
GLIGAR* V
GROVYLE

BATTLE 8
GLIGAR**** V
SWELLOW****

BATTLE 9
METANG V
GLALIE*

Glalie started the battle with Headbutt, and Metang countered with Take Down; both collided but Glalie took most of the damage. The two Pokémon then exchanged several blows and each suffered direct hits, until Metang unleashed a final huge Meteor Mash. At the last moment, Glalie ducked and used spinning Headbutt, which knocked out Metang.

ROUND 3 Tyson* v Ash

BATTLEFIELD TYPE: Grass

BATTLE 1
SCEPTILE** V GLALIE****

Glalie attacked with Ice Beam and Sceptile countered with Solar Beam. Both attacks collided in mid-air, creating an explosion of light, Glalie and Sceptile were both instantly knocked out from the power of the explosion.

BATTLE 2
SHIFTRY V TORKOAL*

Shiftry used Mega Kick and Shadow Ball, both hitting Torkoal, who responded with two Flamethrowers, the second was a direct hit, which knocked Shiftry out.

BATTLE 3
HARIYAMA* V TORKOAL

Torkoal attacked with Flamethrower, which Hariyama evaded with a blast of Arm Thrust. Once Hariyama was within range, it defeated Torkoal with Brick Break.

BATTLE 4
HARIYAMA* V CORPHISH

Corphish opened with Bubble Beam and Hariyama responded with another Brick Break, which Corphish was able to dodge. Corphish and Hariyama blasted towards each other with Crabhammer and Focus Punch. Both attacks collided and caused an explosion, which knocked out Corphish. As Ash had now lost three Pokémon, the field was changed to a Rock field.

BATTLE 5
HARIYAMA V SWELLOW*

Swellow started with Peck attack, but Hariyama caught Swellow's beak between its hands and stopped the attack before slamming Swellow down with a Seismic Toss. While Hariyama charged up for a Focus Punch, Swellow counter-attacked with an Aerial Ace. Hariyama's charged Focus Punch hit the Aerial Ace but Swellow's attack was a direct hit. Hariyama was knocked out.

BATTLE 6

DONPHAN V SWELLOW*

Donphan did Rollout and used a boulder to launch into the air to hit Swellow. Donphan countered with several Rollout attacks which hit Swellow, each hit more powerful than the last. As Donphan attacked with one last Rollout, Swellow managed to stop the attack by catching it with its legs! Swellow then lifted Donphan into the air and dropped it back to the ground, knocking it out.

BATTLE 7

METAGROSS* V SWELLOW

Metagross used Psychic and Swellow defended with Quick Attack but it took damage from its own move. Metagross used Hyper Beam, which defeated Swellow.

BATTLE 8

METAGROSS* V GROVYLE

Grovyle struck Metagross with Bullet Seed and followed up with Leaf Blade but Metagross recovered, taking Grovyle out with Meteor Mash.

BATTLE 9

METAGROSS V PIKACHU*

Pikachu bolted forward with a Thunderbolt, but it had little effect on Metagross. Metagross countered with Psychic, but Pikachu dodged it and used Iron Tail. Pikachu grabbed on to Metagross and used a close-range Thunder, knocking Metagross out.

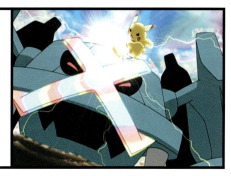

BATTLE 10

MEOWTH* V PIKACHU

After exchanging opening blows, Meowth countered Pikachu's Thunder with Thunderbolt. Both Pokémon did Iron Tail and they collided, evenly matched. Meowth tried Slash and Pikachu used Quick Attack. Pikachu launched Thunder but Meowth defended with Thunderbolt. Again, these equally matched Pokémon did Iron Tail and both got a direct hit. Both managed to stand up, but Pikachu fainted.

BATTLE FRONTIER

KNOWLEDGE SYMBOL

Battle Location:
Battle Factory
(near Cerulean City)
Frontier Brain:
Factory Head Nolan

ARTICUNO V CHARIZARD*

GUTS SYMBOL

Battle Location:
Battle Arena (near
Saffron City)
Frontier Brain:
Arena Tycoon Greta

HARIYAMA AND MEDICHAM V
SNORLAX AND GROVYLE*

TACTICS SYMBOL

Battle Location:
Battle Down (near
Lavender Town)
Frontier Brain:
Dome Ace Tucker

ARCANINE AND SWAMPERT V
SWELLOW AND CORPHISH*

LUCK SYMBOL

Battle Location:
Battle Pike (near
Fuschia City)
Frontier Brain:
Pike Queen Lucy

SEVIPER V DONPHAN*

MILOTIC* V DONPHAN

MILOTIC V PIKACHU*

SPIRITS SYMBOL

Battle Location:
Battle Palace
(Metallica Island)
Frontier Brain:
Palace Mavern Spenser

SHIFTRY V
SCEPTILE*

VENUSAUR* V
HERACROSS

VENUSAUR V
SWELLOW*

CLAYDOL* V
SWELLOW

CLAYDOL V
SCEPTILE*

Ash was back in familiar territory, the Kanto region! But there were still a few surprises. Instead of battling for badges, when you defeat a Frontier Brain you are awarded various symbols. If you win seven symbols, you are offered the chance to become a Frontier Brain.

* winner
** winner after a match withdrawal
*** interrupted battle
**** double KO
***** faints

AGILITY SYMBOL

Battle Location:
Battle Tower
Frontier Brain:
Salon Maiden Anabel

MATCH 1

ALAKAZAM* V TAUROS

ALAKAZAM* V CORPHISH

ALAKAZAM V PIKACHU*

METAGROSS* V PIKACHU

Ash lost for the first time in Battle Frontier. He returned the next day to have another go.

MATCH 2

ALAKAZAM V CORPHISH*

METAGROSS* V CORPHISH

METAGROSS**** V TAUROS****

ESPEON V PIKACHU*

BRAVE SYMBOL

Battle Location:
Battle Pyramid (near Pewter City)
Frontier Brain:
Pyramid King Brandon

Ash became possessed with the King of Pokélantis, and battled Brandon: if Ash wins, he gets all Brandon's Pokémon.

BATTLE 1

REGIROCK* V SCEPTILE

BATTLE 2

DUSCLOPS* V CHARIZARD

DUSCLOPS V BULBASAUR*

NINJASK V SQUIRTLE*

SOLROCK* V SQUIRTLE

SOLROCK**** V BULBASAUR****

REGICE V PIKACHU*

Ash won his final Frontier symbol and became Master of the Battle Frontier!

WELCOME TO THE ...
SINNOH REGION

The Sinnoh region is a vast area separated into two parts by Mount Coronet. There are a lot of freshwater lakes, the most important three are Lake Verity in the west, Lake Acuity in the north and Lake Valor in the east. There is a large forest in the north-west called Eterna Forest.

According to legend, this region was the first in the Pokémon world to have been created. In the nothingness, a single egg came into being, which hatched into Arceus. Arceus created Dialga, Palkia and Giratina, and gave them abilities to control time, space and anti-matter. Later, Arceus created Azelf, Uxie and Mesprit, who were linked to willpower, knowledge and emotion. These Legendary Pokémon are said to live at the bottom of the Sinnoh region's three great lakes. Finally, Arceus created the Sinnoh region.

BADGES ASH WON

In the Sinnoh region, Pokémon Trainers must earn eight badges from Sinnoh gym leaders before they can enter the annual Lily of the Valley Conference.

Gym Leader:
Roark
Oreburgh City Gym
Type: Rock

COAL

Gym Leader:
Gardenia
Eterna Forest Gym
Type: Grass

FOREST

Gym Leader:
Maylene
Veilstone Gym
Type: Fighting

COBBLE

Gym Leader:
Crasher Wake
Pastoria City Gym
Type: Water

FEN

Gym Leader:
Fantina
Hearthome Gym
Type: Ghost

RELIC

Gym Leader:
Byron
Canalave City Gym
Type: Steel

MINE

Gym Leader:
Candice
Snowpoint Gym
Type: Ice

ICICLE

Gym Leader:
Volkner
Sunyshore Gym
Type: Electric

BEACON

POKÉMON SUMMER ACADEMY

WINNER: Ash (Red Team)
The Pokémon Triathalon – consisting of a race across a course to the finish line – was the final event of the Pokémon Summer Academy. Each participant got two Pokémon, but they were picked at random. The first Pokémon helped them through the forest and the second was a Water-type Pokémon, to help them across the lake. During the final dash through a tunnel, Jessie (disguised as Jessalinda) attacked the competitors with her Seviper. Ash rescued Angie from falling down a hole and they raced to the finish line, with Ash winning by a nose!

ASH'S CATCHES

POKÉMON ASH CAUGHT DURING BATTLE FRONTIER AND IN SINNOH

AIPOM

TYPE:
Normal

Aipom was the only Pokémon Ash caught in the Battle Frontier. Later, Ash traded it to Dawn for Buizel, as Aipom loved contests and Buizel loved to battle. When Ash and Pikachu left for Sinnoh region Aipom snuck aboard the boat to travel with him.

STARLY / STARAVIA / STARAPTOR

TYPE:
Normal / Flying

Starly evolved to Staravia to fight against Team Rocket. It also defeated several gym leader's Pokémon. Staravia evolved to Staraptor during a PokéRinger contest and defeated Honchkrow. Staraptor loves to battle and is fierce, fast and proud.

TURTWIG / GROTLE / TORTERRA

TYPE:
Grass / Ground

Turtwig used its speed and small size to defeat Roark's Cranidos. As Grotle, it beat Candice's Sneasel despite the type disadvantage by using precise attacks and defence strategies. As Torterra it became very serious and would always listen to Ash's commands.

Ash's team in the Sinnoh region consisted of Pikachu, Staraptor, Torterra, Buizel, Infernape, Gliscor and Gible. The team included Aipom before it was traded away and replaced by battle-ready Buizel.

CHIMCHAR / MONFERNO / INFERNAPE

TYPE:
Fire / Fighting

Chimchar originally belonged to Paul, who treated it badly and eventually abandoned it. Ash was a much better Trainer and Chimchar's self-esteem improved. After it evolved to become Infernape, it focused on surpassing its limits and enhancing its fighting skills.

GLIGAR / GLISCOR

TYPE:
Ground / Flying

Gligar was afraid of heights and fighting other Pokémon but it gained confidence when it evolved to Gliscor, with the help of a Razor Fang. It defeated Paul's Drapion after perfecting Stone Edge and Fire Fang during its training with McCann.

BUIZEL

TYPE:
Water

Buizel never backs down from a fight and thrives on battling others, even when it is at a disadvantage. It sees fighting opponents who are stronger than it as a way to develop its skills. It has successfully defeated Crasher Wake's Quagsire and Paul's Gastrodon.

GIBLE

TYPE:
Dragon / Ground

When Ash first met Gible, it tried hard to learn Draco Meteor, but the move always failed. When Ash met Gible for a second time, it chose Ash over Barry as its Trainer. Gible finally mastered Draco Meteor during its match with Conway's Shuckle.

PROFESSOR ROWAN

Professor Rowan prefers to be in the field researching the Evolutions and habits of Pokémon. Though known for his stern demeanour, he is always ready with advice to help young Trainers.

Professor Rowan lives in the Sinnoh region. At first he may seem forceful and not that friendly, because he rarely smiles, but it's often just because he is deep in thought. He is good friends with Professor Oak, and they have known each other for a long time.

Rowan enjoys going out into the field to research, to watch, observe and collect data. He often shares his thoughts and findings with other professors, in the hope that together they might come up with new insights into Pokémon.

He specialises in Pokémon Evolution and the habits of Pokémon. As region professor, he gifts new Trainers with their first partner Pokémon, in Sinnoh these are: Chimchar, Piplup and Turtwig. He gives great advice to Trainers when they need it.

DAWN

Before her tenth birthday, Dawn lived in Twinleaf Town with her mother, Johanna, a prize-winning coordinator and Pokémon breeder. Dawn wants to follow in her mother's footsteps.

Dawn is organised, upbeat and cheerful. On her way to meet Professor Rowan and choose her first partner Pokémon, her mum had to stop her taking a HUGE suitcase full of things she thought she might need. Dawn chose Piplup as her first partner Pokémon. She met it after it escaped from Rowan's lab into the woods, they didn't get along at first but bonded after they had to work together to escape some wild Ariados.

HOW DAWN MET ASH

Soon after leaving Sandgem Town, Dawn contacted Professor Rowan to tell him that she had found a lost Pikachu that was being chased by some bad guys called Team Rocket … and had ended up frying her bike with Thunderbolt. Later that day, Ash met up with Rowan to collect his Aipom's Poké Ball, which was sent over by Professor Oak. He informed Ash about his morning call with Dawn, and Ash rushed off to catch up with Dawn and rescue Pikachu. He found them when Ash spotted Pikachu's Volt Tackle move shoot into the sky.

FACTS

- 🔴 Dawn's catchphrase is, 'There's no need to worry!'

- 🔴 She carries her mother's first contest ribbon with her for good luck.

105

TEAM GALACTIC

Unlike the previous villainous teams Ash has come across during his travels, Team Galactic's goals aren't limited to just the world ... they want to create an entire new Pokémon UNIVERSE, which would consume the original one in the process.

Team Galactic hired Team Rocket to steal the Adamant Orb from the Eterna Historical Museum. They stole the Spear Key, which angered a swarm of ancient and mysterious Unown Pokémon. Eventually their plan was revealed: they were using the artifacts they had collected to control the Lake Guardians, Azelf, Uxie and Mesprit, and planned to open a portal to bring Dialga and Palkia through from another dimension. Ash and

his friends rescued the Lake Guardians, but Cyrus, the leader of Team Galactic, got away by jumping through the portal to his new world before it closed forever.

WHAT'S TEAM ROCKET UP TO?

The trio were helping Giovanni expand Team Rocket into a new region, while also being on the lookout for new, rare and powerful Pokémon – but they end up succeeding at neither.

WHO'S JESSALINA?

In Sinnoh, Jessie started to enter contests in disguise as Jessalina where she was actually quite successful, for a change. She won five ribbons: Solaceon, Majolica, Lilypad, Neighbourly and Arrowroot.

JAMES'S CACNEA

Cacnea was the first Pokémon James caught in the Hoenn region. When in the Sinnoh region they met Gardenia, the leader of Eterna City Gym. Gardenia and James fought Ash and Dawn. During the match, Gardenia talked Cacnea through how to perform Drain Punch for the first time. Later, it wasn't able to do the move when James asked it to; Meowth helped to translate that Cacnea said that the first Drain Punch had been a fluke. Gardenia offered to train Cacnea herself so that it could reach its full potential, and though it was heartbreaking for him to let his Pokémon go, James agreed.

JESSIE'S POKÉMON IN SINNOH

WOBBUFFET

DUSTOX

YANMA / YANMMEGA

SEVIPER

JAMES'S POKÉMON IN SINNOH

MIME JR.

CARNIVINE

CHIMECHO

CACNEA

HOW TO MAKE A POKÉMON STRONGER

When Ash first met Paul, he learned that Paul's method was to catch lots of the same Pokémon, check the PokéDex to see which was the strongest one, and then release the weaker ones. He didn't treat the Pokémon as individuals or work hard to get them to be the best they can be; he only saw them as tools for battle. Ash ran into Paul before his battle at Oreburgh City Gym, and he advised Ash to copy him as he'd just won the badge. Ash would never battle or train like Paul with no regard for his Pokémon's emotions or feelings. When Ash met Cynthia from the Elite Four, she told Ash that she also used to train like Paul, but she had learned a different way to train that enhanced the unique strengths and personalities of her Pokémon.

MAKING TURTWIG LISTEN

During a battle with Paul's Stantler, Turtwig (who Ash had only caught recently) was mistrustful of Ash and didn't listen to his commands. Ash lost the battle to Paul and afterwards, Ash took the time to sit down and talk to Turtwig. He handed Turtwig half an apple and Ash told him that he wanted the two of them to be more than just Trainer and Pokémon, that he wanted them to be friends too. During their next battle with Paul, Ash and Turtwig worked much better together as a team, and though they still lost, Ash thanked Turtwig for putting up such a great fight.

In Sinnoh region, Ash met Paul, and the two could not be more opposite. Throughout the time they spent together in Sinnoh region, Ash learned a lot about himself and how he wasn't willing to act as a Trainer.

DISCOVERING WHAT'S BEST FOR YOUR POKÉMON

Dawn and Ash began to notice that Ash's Aipom wanted to perform rather than do battle training with Ash, and Dawn's Buizel was more interested in battling with Ash. It was their friend, Zoe, who first suggested they trade, but Ash and Dawn were hesitant. Both had worked hard with each Pokémon and they had amazing memories with each. The two Trainers ended up battling Team Rocket and it became clear Buizel and Ash were a powerful battling duo. Also, Dawn and Aipom had the flair and performance for contests. The friends agreed that it was in the best interest of their Pokémon for them to switch.

GLISCOR V GLIGAR

On route to Veilstone City, Ash and his friends came across a city that had been overrun by a Gliscor and a pack of Gligar who were eating all the food in sight. Paul caught Gliscor without concern to what would happen to the group without their leader. Ash caught a Gligar that he made friends with during an earlier rescue. Ash and Gligar trained hard together to overcome the Pokémon's poor flying skills. Eventually they challenged Paul and his Gliscor, and lost, which left Gligar with a fear of battling. Paul mocked Ash for keeping a Gligar that could neither fly nor fight. Ash's friend, Gary, helped train Gligar and gave Ash a Razor Fang which would allow it to evolve. When Team Rocket attacked, Gligar decided to evolve to save Ash. Together, Ash and Gliscor were more powerful because of their relationship and the time they had spent together.

TRAINER TALES

The new region brings Ash more opportunity for adventure and getting a few more battles under his belt. Here are some of Ash's exciting moments in the Sinnoh region.

1 ASH AND DAWN FACE THE CHAMP TWINS

When the friends met the Champ Twins, Ash challenged them to a battle, but they only did tag battles and were on a 16-in-a-row hot streak. So Ash and Dawn challenged them together. The first match was Turtwig and Piplup versus Quilava and Croconaw. Ash and Dawn were uncoordinated and argued throughout the battle and ended up attacking each other's Pokémon, so they lost. After a pep talk from Brock and after the two of them teamed up to fight Team Rocket, Ash and Dawn developed a strategy to work together well. At the rematch with the Champ Twins, Dawn and Ash used type advantages and teamwork to finally win.

2 REUNITED WITH OLD FRIENDS

On Mount Coronet, Ash and his friends ran into a Shieldon being hunted by Pokémon Hunter J who had been tasked with capturing it. As they tried to protect it, Gary Oak arrived and saved it with Electivire. Gary explained that he and Professor Rowan were working on an environmental project to create a Shieldon reserve. Oak intended to move the Pokémon to a safer location and Ash offered to help. But Hunter J captured it and tried to deliver it to her buyer. Ash and Gary teamed up to fight her and launched a battle. In the confusion, Ash freed Shieldon from its cage. Gary thanked his friend for helping him get the Pokémon to safety.

3 REBUILDING A FRIEND'S CONFIDENCE

When Ash met Maylene, the leader of Veilstone City Gym, she had recently been defeated by Paul, who called her the weakest gym leader he'd ever faced. This knocked Maylene's confidence massively, especially as she had just taken over leadership of the gym from her grandfather. Her Lucario was angry with Maylene for refusing to lead the gym and was trying to get her to go back to her duties. Maylene ran away, but Dawn followed her and the two talked through their doubts and confidence in themselves. They found strength from each other and decided to battle the next day.

4 ASH CAN USE AURA!

When Ash came across a Riolu in the forest, he had a strange feeling. He looked at the Pokédex entry and found that Riolu is sensitive to Aura, an energy that allows some Pokémon and people empathic and telepathic abilities. In Riolu, this sensitivity becomes stronger when it is afraid. Later on, Ash was able to use Aura to sense what Riolu was feeling and thinking about, and discovered Riolu was lost. Ash promised Riolu he would get it back to its Trainer and its kingdom. Meanwhile, in an effort to capture Riolu, Pokémon Hunter J started a wildfire in the forest with her Salamence. Ash found out where J was taking Riolu using their Aura connection, and set off to rescue it along with Pokémon Ranger Kellyn. They managed to reunite it with its Trainer.

ASH, PAUL AND CHIMCHAR

When Ash signed up for the Hearthome Tag Team Battle, he was not thrilled to learn that Paul was going to be his partner for the whole three days.

'In a tag battle, the real key to success is to create the spirit of partnership between both Trainers and their Pokémon to learn to truly rely on each other …'

Can Ash and Paul put their rivalry and differences aside so they can win?

Before their first battle, Paul declared that the only reason he had signed up was to meet Fire-type Pokémon. His strategy for strengthening his Chimchar was to make it face more powerful Fire types, as he said, 'Getting hurt from the weaknesses you have makes you stronger.'

BATTLE 1

| PIKACHU AND CHIMCHAR* | V | RHYDON AND MAGMAR |

Ash and Paul didn't communicate at all during this match, and Ash was alarmed when Paul had Chimchar face Rhydon's Surf with Flame Wheel. Thinking on his feet, Ash told Pikachu to do Iron Tail to cut through the water and knock out Rhydon, which saved Chimchar from being hit too.

To take out Magmar, Ash used Pikachu's Volt Tackle in combination with Chimchar's Dig. After the match, Ash argued again that

the two would be better working together as a team, but Paul refused.

LATER ON ...

Ash caught up with Paul training his Chimchar before their second battle. Paul had put his Murkrow, Ursaring, Elekid and

Torterra against Chimchar to strengthen it and activate its Blaze ability. Ash thought that he was pushing Chimchar too hard and should be concentrating on developing its strengths instead.

Ash stopped the training and took the injured Chimchar to the Pokémon Centre to be healed, and Nurse Joy said it should not battle the next day.

BATTLE 2

TURTWIG AND CHIMCHAR*

V

METAGROSS AND ZANGOOSE

Despite the warning, Paul chose Chimchar to battle anyway. Paul had Chimchar use Flame Wheel against Turtwig, its own teammate. When Chimchar was too afraid to fight, Paul checked out of the match and refused to give Chimchar any more commands, so Ash took over on his own and scored a surprise victory.

After the match, Paul set Chimchar free, saying it was too weak. Ash offered Chimchar a place on his team.

BATTLE 3

STARAVIA AND TORTERRA*

V

CROAGUNK AND FARFETCH'D

This battle was against Brock and Holly. Ash let Chimchar out of its Poké Ball to watch the match. Ash and Paul argued constantly throughout the battle, and Paul's Staravia accidentally injured Ash's Torterra.

Despite Brock and Holly being the stronger team, Ash and Paul won due to their Pokémon having such powerful attacks.

BATTLE 4

CHIMCHAR AND ELEKID* V BUIZEL AND HERACROSS

This battle was against Dawn and Conway. Ash begged Paul to work with him as a team otherwise they would lose, but Paul didn't seem to care, so Ash decided to attack alone. Ash and Paul were losing, until Elekid evolved into Electabuzz, giving the team the extra power they needed to knock out Buizel and Heracross, ultimately winning the Hearthome Tag Battle.

The win came despite Ash and Paul not working together once. Paul called Chimchar's Flamethrower pathetic but Ash said Chimchar was awesome and they were only going to grow stronger together.

The rivals parted, until their next battle ...

CHIMCHAR V URSARING

When Paul and Ash next met, Ash and his Pokémon had a lot of scores to settle. Ash brought out Chimchar against Paul's Ursaring – one of the Pokémon that Paul had used to hurt and bully Chimchar.

After being covered in a pile of rocks by Ursaring's Hammer Arm, Chimchar was able to activate its Blaze ability. This was enough to take out Ursaring, but Chimchar was deeply affected. In the end, only Ash could calm it down with a hug.

BATTLE BREAKDOWN

THE SINNOH REGION GYM

MATCH 1

OREBURGH CITY GYM

COAL BADGE

ROARK V ASH

Ash first battled Roark for the badge and lost ... Ash's first battle loss in Sinnoh region. He was battle-ready for the rematch! The gym rules were a 3-on-3 battle, where only the challenger can make substitutions.

BATTLE 1	BATTLE 2	BATTLE 3

CRANIDOS* V AIPOM	CRANIDOS** V PIKACHU	CRANIDOS V TURTWIG*

ETERNA CITY GYM

FOREST BADGE

GARDENIA V ASH

The first time Ash battled Gardenia he lost, so they promised each other that this official gym battle would be one to remember! It was a 3-on-3 battle.

BATTLE 1	BATTLE 2
 V	 V
CHERUBI** V TURTWIG	CHERUBI V STARAVIA*

VEILSTONE CITY GYM

COBBLE BADGE

MAYLENE V ASH

Maylene had regained her confidence so accepted Ash's 3-on-3 challenge, which ended in a draw. In the event of a tie, a gym leader chooses the winner. Gardenia gave Ash the badge for a good match.

BATTLE 1	BATTLE 2
 V	
MACHOKE V STARAVIA*	MEDITITE** V STARAVIA

PASTORIA CITY GYM

FEN BADGE

CRASHER WAKE V ASH

Ash's Buizel and Pikachu had a big falling-out just before the match. This was a 3-on-3 battle, with only the challenger being allowed to substitute.

BATTLE 1	BATTLE 2
 V	
GYARADOS V PIKACHU*	QUAGSIRE** V TURTWIG

Ash needed eight badges from Sinnoh League gyms to enter the Lily of the Valley Conference. Again, Ash left his Pokémon in the Oak Corral so he could have a new team. He took Pikachu, obviously, but Aipom stowed away with him too.

* winner
** winner after a match withdrawal
*** interrupted battle
**** double KO
***** faints

MATCH 2

BATTLE 4	BATTLE 5	BATTLE 1	BATTLE 2	BATTLE 3	BATTLE 4	BATTLE 5

| ONIX* V TURTWIG | ONIX* V PIKACHU | ONIX V PIKACHU* | GEODUDE V AIPOM* | RAMPARDOS* V AIPOM | RAMPARDOS* V PIKACHU | RAMPARDOS V TURTWIG* |

BATTLE 3 | **BATTLE 4** | **BATTLE 5** | **BATTLE 6**

| TURTWIG* | STARAVIA | TURTWIG | TURTWIG* | ROSERADE* | TURTWIG | ROSERADE | AIPOM* |

BATTLE 3 | **BATTLE 4** | **BATTLE 5** | **BATTLE 6** | **BATTLE 7**

| MEDITITE** | CHIMCHAR | MEDITITE | STARAVIA* | LUCARIO* | STARAVIA | LUCARIO* | CHIMCHAR | LUCARIO* | BUIZEL* |

BATTLE 3 | **BATTLE 4** | **BATTLE 5** | **BATTLE 6**

| QUAGSIRE | BUIZEL* | FLOATZEL** | BUIZEL | FLOATZEL** | PIKACHU | FLOATZEL | BUIZEL* |

117

HEARTHOME CITY GYM

RELIC BADGE

FANTINA V ASH

Ash lost his first battle with Fantina after her Drifblim kept putting his team to sleep with Hypnosis. Now, with a special counter-tactic developed, Ash was ready to challenge for the Relic Badge. This was a 3-on-3 battle.

BATTLE 1

GENGAR V BUIZEL*

BATTLE 2

MISMAGIUS V CHIMCHAR*

CANALAVE CITY GYM

MINE BADGE

BYRON V ASH

Byron's love of defence tactics didn't make this an easy battle. Roark, the gym leader from Oreburgh City, turned up to referee this 3-on-3 battle.

BATTLE 1

BRONZOR V CHIMCHAR*

BATTLE 2

STEELIX* V BUIZEL

SNOWPOINT CITY GYM

ICICLE BADGE

CANDICE V ASH

Ash comes out fighting with Grass types, which have a type disadvantage against Candice's Ice types. The challenge for the Icicle Badge is a 4-on-4 battle, with only the challenger able to make substitutions.

BATTLE 1

SNEASEL V GROTLE*

BATTLE 2

MEDICHAM V STARAPTOR*

SUNYSHORE CITY GYM

BEACON BADGE

VOLKNER V ASH

The gym was badly damaged by Team Rocket, and Volkner promised Ash he would be his first battle when the gym was repaired. The 3-on-3 battle began, with only the challenger able to make substitutions.

BATTLE 1

ELECTIVIRE* V TORTERRA

BATTLE 2

ELECTIVIRE V PIKACHU*

BATTLE 3

DRIFBLIM* **V** PIKACHU

BATTLE 4

DRIFBLIM* **V** BUIZEL

BATTLE 5

DRIFBLIM **V** CHIMCHAR*

BATTLE 3

STEELIX **V** CHIMCHAR*

BATTLE 4

BASTIODON* **V** CHIMCHAR

BATTLE 5

BASTIODON* **V** GLISCOR

BATTLE 3

SNOVER* V
GLISCOR

BATTLE 4

SNOVER V
CHIMCHAR*

BATTLE 5

ABOMASNOW** V
CHIMCHAR

BATTLE 6

ABOMASNOW* V
STARAPTOR

BATTLE 7

ABOMASNOW* V
GROTLE

BATTLE 8

ABOMANOW V
CHIMCHAR*

BATTLE 3

JOLTEON **V** INFERNAPE*

BATTLE 4

LUXRAY* **V** PIKACHU

BATTLE 5

LUXRAY **V** INFERNAPE*

LILY OF THE VALLEY CONFERENCE

The annual Lily of the Valley Conference takes place on Lily of the Valley Island. After an initial round, 64 participants then enter the Preliminary Rounds. The first two rounds are 3-on-3 smaller arena matches with the third round in the main arena. In the final rounds, the match-ups are reshuffled and the top eight are in 6-on-6 battles.

* winner
** winner after a match withdrawal
*** interrupted battle
**** double KO
***** faints

MATCH 1 Nando v Ash

Ash had met Nando on his travels before, and the old friends looked forward to a good battle together.

BATTLE 1 ROSERADE V STARAPTOR*

BATTLE 2 ARMALDO* V STARAPTOR

BATTLE 3 ARMALDO**** V QUILAVA****

BATTLE 4 KRICKETUNE V HERACROSS*

MATCH 2 Conway v Ash

This was a clash of two opposing battle styles: Conway's planned approach versus Ash's 'in the moment' style.

BATTLE 1 SHUCKLE** V NOCTOWL

BATTLE 5 LICKILICKY V NOCTOWL*
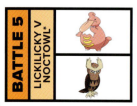

BATTLE 2 SHUCKLE** V DONPHAN

BATTLE 6 DUSKNOIR* V NOCTOWL

BATTLE 3 SHUCKLE V GIBLE*

BATTLE 7 DUSKNOIR* V DONPHAN

BATTLE 4 LICKILICKY** V GIBLE

BATTLE 8 DUSKNOIR V GIBLE*

MATCH 3 Paul v Ash

This quarter-final battle was a chance to settle the long-standing rivalry between Ash and Paul once and for all.

BATTLE 1
AGGRON V PIKACHU

Pikachu used Thunderbolt to evade Aggron's Metal Sound. Pikachu charged with Volt Tackle but Aggron countered with Flash Cannon, Pikachu was out.

BATTLE 2
AGGRON V INFERNAPE*

Infernape's Flare Blitz was matched by Aggron's Flash Cannon. Aggron defended with Rock Head, but was sent flying with Infernape's fast Mach Punch.

BATTLE 3
GASTRODON V STARAPTOR

Paul had Gastrodon use Muddy Water as a counter-shield, one of Ash's strategies! When Gastrodon had Staraptor pinned to the ground it shot Water Pulse straight up into the air and the attack gathered speed and power. To free Staraptor, Ash told it to do Close Combat at the ground, and it evaded the attack. Finally, Gastrodon did Ice Beam before Ash recalled Staraptor.

BATTLE 4
GASTRODON V BUIZEL*

Buizel attacked by turning Gastrodon's own Ice Beam into a solid Ice Aqua Jet. Gastrodon used Body Slam, but Buizel's Ice Punch to Gastrodon's belly knocked him out.

BATTLE 5
DRAPION* V BUIZEL

Paul's counter-attack started in full force. Drapion used Toxic Spikes, so when Buizel landed on the field, it was poisoned and Drapion knocked it out with Pin Missile.

BATTLE 6
DRAPION* V STARAPTOR

This match was over quickly when Drapion plucked Staraptor out of the sky, attacked it with Cross Poison and slammed it into the ground still laced with Toxic Spikes.

BATTLE 7
DRAPION* V TORTERRA

Toxic Spikes weakened Torterra from the beginning, and after the two exchanged some powerful moves, Drapion took out Torterra with a Pin Missile attack.

BATTLE 8
NINJASK V GLISCOR

Ninjask's Agility and Speed Boost ability quickly overwhelmed Gliscor who tried to counter with Stone Edge and Fire Fang. Ash recalled Gliscor as he was poisoned by the Toxic Spikes.

BATTLE 9
NINJASK V INFERNAPE*

To rid the field of Toxic Spikes, Ash told Infernape to perform an underground Flare Blitz. Ninjask was damaged so Infernape used Mach Punch to knock it out.

BATTLE 10
FROSLASS V PIKACHU*

Froslass's Hail and Snow Cloak left Pikachu unable to land any attacks. Froslass froze Pikachu with Ice Beam, but Pikachu used Volt Tackle to burst out and knock Froslass out.

BATTLE 11
DRAPION V GLISCOR*

Gliscor used its agility and speed to dodge Drapion's attacks and kept out of range. When it was close enough to use Fire Fang, it hit and burned Drapion and knocked it out.

BATTLE 12
ELECTRIVIRE* V GLISCOR

Paul was on his last Pokémon … but Electric-type attacks had no effect on Gliscor, though it had taken a lot of damage. Electrivire used Thunder to hit Gliscor with rocks.

BATTLE 13
ELECTRIVIRE* V PIKACHU

Both Pokémon only had a few non-Electric-type moves to use. Unfortunately, Ash made a mistake in his strategy, Pikachu got too close and was hit by Brick Break.

BATTLE 14
ELECTRIVIRE V INFERNAPE*

After the two battle to the point of near exhaustion, Infernape fell to the ground. The referee was about to call the match when Infernape's Blaze ability kicked in and it proved too powerful for Electrivire, who was knocked out after getting hit by Flare Blitz.

This was the first time Ash had beaten Paul.

MATCH 4 Tobias v Ash

Ash had made it to the top four in a Championship League final. Tobias's team had the Mythical Pokémon, Darkrai.

BATTLE 1 — DARKRAI* V HERACROSS

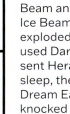

Heracross's Hyper Beam and Darkrai's Ice Beam collided and exploded. But Darkrai used Dark Void and sent Heracross to sleep, then unleashed Dream Eater and knocked it out.

BATTLE 2 — DARKRAI* V TORKOAL

Torkoal's opening Flamethrower was ineffective against Darkrai, who aimed an overwhelming Dark Pulse at the same time, knocking Torkoal out in one move.

BATTLE 3 — DARKRAI* V GIBLE

Gible managed to get some hits in on Darkrai, including Dark Smash. After Darkrai dodged Draco Meteor, it hit Gible with a Dark Pulse and the battle was over.

BATTLE 4 — DARKAI V SCEPTILE*

When Darkrai used Dark Void, it looked like this battle would be over, but Sceptile managed to shake off the Dream Eater attack and used Leaf Blade, which knocked out Darkrai. Sceptile was the first Pokémon in the entire tournament to defeat Darkrai.

BATTLE 5 — LATIOS* V SCEPTILE

Sceptile attacks with another Leaf Blade, but Latios counters with Giga Impact. Both moves smash together, causing an explosion and Sceptile faints.

WELCOME TO THE ...
UNOVA REGION

The Unova region is far away from the four other large regions, and the Pokémon that live there are different from those of the Kanto, Johto, Hoenn and Sinnoh regions. So is the climate, as spring, summer, autumn and winter only last thirty days, so each season happens three times a year. Unova is known for embodying two opposites: bustling cities and quiet forests.

The Unova region is the setting for many great mythological stories. Over 2,500 years ago, the argument between two brothers split a dragon into two; Reshiram and Zekrom. The dragons fought, but neither could defeat the other. Eventually their battles destroyed Unova. It is believed that later, one of the brothers and their dragon created the Relic Castle and it became the new seat of the Unova people and their Pokémon.

BADGES ASH WON

In Unova, as in other regions, Trainers must earn eight badges from Unova gym leaders before they can enter the Unova League, the Vertress Conference.

Gym Leader:
Chili
Striaton City Gym
Type: Fighting

TRIO

Gym Leader:
Lenora
Nacrene City Gym
Type: Normal

BASIC

Gym Leader:
Elesa
Nimbasa City Gym
Type: Bug

INSECT

Gym Leader:
Burgh
Castelia City Gym
Type: Electric

BOLT

Gym Leader:
Clay
Driftveil City Gym
Type: Ground

QUAKE

Gym Leader:
Skyla
Mistralton City Gym
Type: Flying

JET

Gym Leader:
Brycen
Icirrrus City Gym
Type: Ice

FREEZE

Gym Leader:
Roxie
Virbank City Gym
Type: Poison

TOXIC

COMPETITIONS

The Pokémon World Tournament Junior Cup was held in Lacunosa Town. The battles are timed with ten minutes on the clock. Sixteen competitors enter, with the winner receiving a gold trophy and the chance to battle the Unova League champion, Alder.

Ash finished the tournament in second place to Trip.

The final battle saw Trip's Serperior versus Ash's Pignite. Even though Pignite had the type advantage, Serperior's speed meant it dodged

every one of Pignite's attacks, until it got hit by Solar Beam. An exhausted Pignite still got up and used Fire Pledge, but Serperior dodged again and used Frenzy Plant which knocked Pignite out.

ASH'S CATCHES

Ash caught quite a few Pokémon in the Unova region, which meant he regularly rotated his core team of six, as well as including his old and loyal friend, Pikachu.

PIDOVE / TRANQUIL / UNFEZANT

TYPE:
Normal / Flying

Unfezant is a very helpful Pokémon who is always happy to go the extra mile during training. It is very confident, but not confrontational and will try and retreat first rather than attack. Ash caught Unfezant when it was a Pidove. As Unfezant, it defeated Cameron's Riolu in the Vertress Conference despite its type disadvantage.

OSHAWOTT

TYPE:
Water

Oshawott originally belonged to Professor Juniper as one of the three first partner Pokémon, but it took an interest in Ash and followed him out of the lab. Oshawott was afraid of water – strange for a Water type! – but it got over its fear when it beat a wild Palpitoad. It fought bravely against Cameron's Hydreigon. It can also come out of its Poké Ball of its own accord.

TEPIG / PIGNITE

TYPE:
Fire / Fighting

Just like Charizard and Infernape, Tepig was abandoned by a cruel Trainer who thought that it was too weak. Ash rescued it as a Tepig, and it evolved into Pignite during a battle with its previous Trainer. Pignite defeated Cameron's Hydreigon in the quarter-finals of the Unova League and won the Sumo Tournament by knocking out Rodney's Golurk.

SNIVY

TYPE:
Grass

Snivy is a fierce competitor and takes each battle seriously. It tends not to show any emotions except when it's battling. Snivy battled against Trip's Servine and Georgia's Pawniard and won. Snivy had quite a few disagreements with Iris's Emolga. With Snivy being especially annoyed every time Emolga used its cuteness to get what it wanted.

SCRAGGY

TYPE:
Dark / Fighting

From the moment Scraggy hatched from an egg, it showed itself to be headstrong and confident – this often landed it in trouble! It began by headbutting a tree full of Galvantula, and had to be saved by Ash and Iris. It became best friends with Iris's Pokémon, Axew. Scraggy has beaten Cilan's Axew twice and faced a wild Garbodor during his walk with Gothita.

SEWADDLE / SWADLOON / LEAVANNY

TYPE:
Bug / Grass

Sewaddle, at all stages of Evolution, is highly competitive and has a strong passion for battling, always trying its hardest to defeat its opponent. After evolving into Leavanny, it adopts a more caring nature and often acts like a parent to the other Pokémon. Leavanny was able to knock out Roxie's Koffing despite having a type disadvantage.

PALPITOAD

TYPE:
Water / Ground

Ash got off to a rough start with Palpitoad, accidentally trespassing in its territory causing it to attack. Ash used Oshawott to capture this feisty Pokémon and add it to his catches. Palpitoad is physically tough, as shown in the gym battle with Elesa and in the battle against Stephan. Palpitoad can use a Poison-type move even though it is a Water and Ground type.

ROGGENROLA / BOLDORE

TYPE:
Rock

As a Roggenrola, it was shown to be very resourceful; for example using its Flash Cannon attack to destroy falling boulders. It was a tough catch for Ash. Roggenrola also cares deeply for others and goes out of its way to ensure their safety, such as the lengths it went to save the other Roggenrola from Team Rocket. Boldore retained its friendly nature.

SANDILE / KROKOROK / KROOKODILE

TYPE:
Ground / Dark

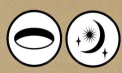

As a Sandile, it was determined to beat Ash's Pikachu. After losing in several battles, it evolved to Krokorok in an attempt to finally win, but still lost. As a Krookodile, it became much faster and stronger. It keeps its trademark sunglasses throughout its Evolutions, and once, when it lost them, it lost all its confidence and became very shy.

PROFESSOR JUNIPER

Professor Juniper is the professor for the Unova region. Professor Oak thinks she is one of the most important researchers in the Pokémon world.

Juniper's research focuses on the origins of Pokémon. She invents and builds her own machines to help with her studies, including a Pokémon Trading Device. Her most incredible device is the Pokémon Restoration Machine, which harnessed Musharna's Dream Energy to bring the ancient Archen back to life from its fossil.

Juniper's main lab is in Nuvema Town, but her research takes her all over the region. As region professor, she gifts new Trainers with their first partner Pokémon, in Unova these are: Tepig, Snivy or Oshawatt. Her father is world-renowned archaeologist, Professor Cedric Juniper.

ASH AND OSHAWOTT

A few days after travelling side by side, Ash asked Oshawott to join his team, but after tossing it the Poké Ball, Ash realised that Oshawott was one of Juniper's Pokémon. Ash called her to let her know and she was so moved by Oshawott's new bond with Ash that she gifted him its Poké Ball.

IRIS

CILAN

Iris is from the Village of Dragons and her dream is to become a Dragon Master. She left home to learn and explore and became Ash's guide through the Unova region.

HOW IRIS MET ASH

Ash was running through the forest, imagining what Pokémon he might discover first, when he spotted something in a bush. He threw a Poké Ball at it … but it turned out to be Iris! She was so excited to see a Pikachu, as these are very rare in Unova and aren't found in the wild. Eventually Iris became Champion of the Unova League and was one of the Masters Eight in the World Coronation Series.

Cilan is one of the gym leaders of Striaton City, along with his brothers Chili and Cress; the three of them are triplets. Cilan is also a Pokémon connoisseur, which is someone who specialises in identifying compatibility between Trainers and Pokémon.

HOW CILAN MET ASH

While he was running errands one day, Cilan ran into Iris and Ash. He noticed Iris's Axew and remarked on how they were  perfect partners. He also got excited to see a Pikachu in real life. When Ash explained he was there to challenge at the gym, Cilan happily offered to show them the way. It wasn't until much later when they were in a cafe that Cilan revealed himself to be one of the three gym leaders.

After Ash's match with his brothers, Chili and Cress, Cilan decided to join Ash on his adventures so he could experience different cities and ultimately improve his connoisseur skills.

WHAT'S TEAM ROCKET UP TO?

When the trio reach the Unova region, they are fed up with being the joke, so they decide to get serious! They have new uniforms, a new mission statement and new vehicles!

NEW POKÉMON

When the trio asked Giovanni's assistant to send Pokémon to help them achieve their missions, they were told that using Pokémon not from the Unova region will mean they stand out too much. So both Jessie and James had to catch their team from scratch.

JESSIE'S POKÉMON IN UNOVA

WOOBAT

FRILLISH

JAMES'S POKÉMON IN UNOVA

YAMASK

AMOONGUSS

The new serious trio actually started being more than just a mild nuisance to Ash and his friends! They completed several missions for Giovanni, and even located the mythical Pokémon, Meloetta. Eventually the trio teamed up with Ash to stop Team Plasma's evil plans, but even then, they couldn't resist trying to steal Pikachu!

NEW MOTTO!

The new serious trio have a new motto to match their lofty, evil ambitions.

What a question, twerpish indeed!
We'll answer these questions when we feel the need!
Bringing the blinding white light of evil into the future!
Thrusting the hammer of justice down on to the black darkness of the universe!
Carving our names in the Rock of Eternity.
The fiery destroyer, Jessie!
And with thunderous emotion, I am James!
Wisest of the wise, Meowth!
Now gather under the name of Team Rocket!

TEAM PLASMA

At first glance, the goal of Team Plasma seemed to be to 'liberate' all Pokémon from their Trainers – they achieved this by going around the region and either tricking Trainers into giving up their Pokémon, or by stealing them.

Team Plasma's mysterious leader, Ghetsis, revealed his true motive – to control the whole Unova region and rule over it as the only human to have Pokémon at his side. The particular Pokémon he wanted to control and be at his command was Reshiram, the Legendary Dragon- and Fire-type Pokémon.

RESHIRAM

After Team Plasma successfully stole the Light Stone from the White Ruins, Ghetsis performed a ritual that resurrected Reshiram from a stone. Using the Pokémon Control Device, invented by Colress, Ghetsis took control over Reshiram … until Ash and Pikachu helped it fight back! It destroyed the machine and all of Team Plasma were arrested by the International Police.

TEAM PLASMA'S LEADER: GHETSIS

PRACTISE YOUR BASICS

When Ash first arrived in the Unova region, Pikachu was zapped by a bolt of blue lightning from the Legendary Pokémon, Zekrom. Pikachu's cheeks started sparking! After a check-up at Professor Juniper's lab, Pikachu was given the all-clear. When Ash later battled Tripp, Ash thought it would be an easy win. Tripp and Snivy had never taken part in a battle before. But for some reason Pikachu couldn't do any electric attacks and was slower than normal, so the battle felt very much like Ash's first time too! Ash and Pikachu lost, and Ash ran back to the lab to help Pikachu. Eventually Juniper realised that Pikachu was overcharged, and a second mysterious bolt from Zekrom seemed to cure Pikachu. Ash realised that no matter how much he'd learned or experienced, it's always important to brush up on the basics of battling.

KROOKODILE'S MOVE SET

When training his newly evolved Krookodile, Ash learned an important lesson in how to balance out a Pokémon's set of moves. Krookodile was so effective in battle because it had a wide variety of attacks, including those from types other that its own. This gave it the upper hand against more opponents. His move set was: Dragon Claw (Dragon type), Dig (Ground type), Aerial Ace (Flying type), Crunch (Dark type) and Stone Edge (Rock type). When Ash told Krookodile to use Aerial Ace in a battle against Stephan and Sawk, everyone was surprised! This unexpected move countered three of its own type weaknesses; Flying, Bug and Grass. Krookodile's well-rounded move set and strategy in battle really showed Ash's growth as a balanced and strong Trainer.

Unova is a fresh start for Ash and he gets the opportunity to both embrace what he's learned so far, and also strengthen his basics in a way that really helps him become a better Pokémon Trainer and friend.

FRIENDSHIP BETWEEN POKÉMON

Ash found himself on familiar ground when he met Fire-type Tepig, but that didn't mean there weren't new lessons to learn! Tepig was abandoned by its original Trainer, Shamus, and tied to a post but it escaped. Later, Tepig volunteered to help Ash rescue Pikachu from Team Rocket and afterwards, Ash asked it to join his team. At the Battle Club, Tepig recognised Shamus and happily ran over to see him but was rejected again. Angered at Shamus's actions, Ash challenged him to battle. Tepig froze in the battle against its former Trainer but, after watching his friend, Snivy, take two powerful hits, Tepig finally jumped into action. When their opponents countered, Snivy pushed Tepig out of the way and took major damage. This act of friendship gave Tepig the courage to evolve into Pignite and win the battle. Ash learned how important the bonds between his Pokémon were.

STAND UP FOR YOURSELF

Skyla, the leader of Mistralton City Gym, had an unusual way of accepting challenges. She would have challengers participate in what she called an 'Air Battle', where she played the battle out in her head. She matched up her Pokémon against the opponents and making decisions on their strengths and weaknesses, she would award the badge based on this, with no real-life battle taking place. Skyla was confident she would beat Ash but he was determined to prove her wrong. Ash and his Tranquill were at a major disadvantage against Skyla's Swanna, but Tranquill came out fighting and dealt some blows, until it was knocked out of the sky by Hurricane. With some encouragement from Ash, Tranquill evolved into Unfezant and an intense and fast-paced aerial battle took place. Unfezant landed Aerial Ace to win. Skyla enjoyed the match so much, she decided to change her methods and not do 'Air Battles' from now on, and Ash learned to stick to his guns.

TRAINER TALES

There's a new adventure around every corner in the Unova region! With a strong team of Pokémon to hand, and an old friend who joins his team, here are some exciting tales.

1 OSHAWOTT AND ITS SCALCHOP

Oshawott have a weapon that grows on their tummies called a scalchop. They use this mighty shell-shaped object to defend and attack – it can stop powerful moves like Bullet Seed and Solar Beam in their tracks! During an epic battle with Stephan's Blitzle, its Double Kick knocked Oshawott's scalchop into the air and it disappeared into the forest. Oshawott lost all its confidence and began to lose the battle, so it ran away into the forest to find its missing weapon. After Oshawott couldn't find it, Ash and the gang jumped into action and tried hard to make Oshawott a new alternative. A Lapapa Berry turned out to be no match for Pikachu's Thunderbolt, so Cilan's Dwebble made a HUGE scalchop out of rock. This worked better at defending against powerful attacks, but was too heavy for Oshawott to carry. To help his friend, Ash helped Oshawott train throughout the night, working on its speed. The next day, Oshawott was ready to battle and took on Blitzle again, and won even without its scalchop!

2 CHARIZARD RETURNS!

While at a Kanto region culture festival, Ash started to reminisce about his friend, Charizard. He recalled it for his Unova region team. As soon as Charizard was let out of its Poké Ball, it lovingly burned Ash with Flamethrower, as it had done since it was a Charmander. When it laid eyes on Iris's Dragonite, the two wanted to battle each other immediately. To show its strength, Charizard hit Dragonite hard with its Dragon-type move, Dragon Tail, which sent Dragonite flying backwards, gaining its respect.

3 WOKEN UP BY A UFO!

One night, Ash and his pals were woken up by a UFO! When they chatted about this in town the next day, the townspeople told them that they have all had visions of outer space. Professor Icarus, who studied UFOs, lived nearby and so the friends travelled to talk to him about these visions; Cilan was a huge fan of his! On the way to the professor's house, the friends had another vision – a vision of danger! At the lab, they met a mysterious Pokémon called Elgyem who lived at Icarus's house. It turned out Elgyem had been creating the visions everyone has seen and had been using Telekenesis to fly the UFO Professor Icarus built through the sky! The out-of-this-world mystery was solved and Elgyem continued to live happily with Professor Icarus.

4 IRIS'S EMOLGA BECOMES A TEAM ROCKET MEMBER?!

Iris's Emolga certainly has a temper, especially when it comes to food! After having a little falling-out with Axew, which led to Axew getting hurt, Iris got cross with Emolga. Emolga decided to run away … and joined Team Rocket! When Emolga first came across Team Rocket, it took down all their Pokémon single-handedly but the trio eventually thought they'd convinced Emolga to join them. The little Pokémon had other plans and only joined to prove a point to Iris. Emolga even had its own part in the famous Team Rocket motto! Emolga's time with the trio was short-lived though, as Iris and Ash came to its rescue and they all went home.

Ash has seen and spotted a few Legendary Pokémon on his journey throughout the Pokémon world, but this is the first time he encountered some properly. Ash and his friends were looking for the Revival Herbs from the Milos Islands so Driftveil City's gym leader would accept his challenge to battle. While they were on their quest, they ran into a local called Lewis, who asked for their help to summon the fertility god, Landorus. All the Revival Herbs on the island had dried up due to the lack of rainfall and some of the Grass-type Pokémon were getting sick. Lewis performed a rain-dance ritual, and ended up summoning the chaotic Pokémon, Tornadus and Thundurus. These two Legendaries had been rivals for a very long time so they started to battle each other, destroying the island as they fought. Ash, Iris, Cilan and their Pokémon did their best to try and stop the Legendaries, but they were just too powerful. With Iris's help, Landorus was summoned, to protect the island, as the guardian of Milos Island as well as

being the only being powerful enough to stop Thundurus and Tornadus. As an epic battle between the three Legendries continues in the sky, Team Rocket were plotting to capture the Legendary Pokémon – they waited for them to tire themselves out and then swooped in to capture them. The friends end up freeing the Legendries and Team Rocket blasted off again. But Landorus was injured, so Lewis gave it the last remaining Revival Herb and it defeated Tornadus and Thundurus. Rain returned to the island and Ash took the Revival Herbs back to Driftveil City.

TRIP

BIANCA

Ash's time in the Unova region was definitely his rivals era. He came across so many rivals on his journey, here are some of the best ones.

TRIP
Ash lost his first Unova region battle against Trip and Snivy, and from this, a rivalry was born. Trip is the opposite to Ash – he isn't interested in making friends and doesn't have time for emotions! The early loss to Trip motivates Ash to work hard in the Unova region so he can finally beat him.

BIANCA
She has lots of energy and is incredibly sweet and kind. She repeatedly ran into Ash, quite literally knocking him flying through the air into water every time their paths crossed. Bianca also had some great battle wins against Trip and Georgia.

STEPHAN
However you pronounce his name, he doesn't mind, as long as you are asking him to battle! Stephan's friendly rivalry with Ash really helped the two of them push each other to new heights. Even when he lost to Ash in the semi-finals of the Vertress Conference, he cheered Ash on from the stands in his next match.

CAMERON
Cameron is full of energy, very unorganised and prone to mistakes; he turned up to his Vertress Conference battle with Ash with only five Pokémon as he had forgotten that he needed six! Cameron is proof though that you should never underestimate someone, especially someone with the desire to win.

VIRGIL
Virgil is part of the Pokémon Rescue Squad and is an Eevee expert! He met Ash and Iris when he rescued them from a rockslide outside of Vertress City. He is the eventual winner of the Unova League.

STEPHAN

CAMERON

VIRGIL

BATTLE BREAKDOWN

THE UNOVA REGION GYM

STRIATON CITY GYM

TRIO BADGE

1. *CHILI V ASH*
2. *CRESS V ASH*
3. *CILAN V ASH*

This gym is run by triplet brothers, Chili, Cress and Cilan. Usually a Trainer picks one of them to battle, but Ash challenges all three!

NACRENE CITY GYM

BASIC BADGE

LENORA V ASH

Ash had battled Lenora before and lost. But after training with Don George's Battle Club, he challenges her again. This is a 2-on-2 with Lenora calling out her Pokémon beforehand.

BATTLE 1

 V

HERDIER*** V TEPIG***

Herdier uses Roar, which forces a Pokémon change.

NIMBASA CITY GYM

INSECT BADGE

ELESA V ASH

Ash spent a lot of time strategising before this tough 3-on-3 battle.

BATTLE 1

 V

TEPIG*** V PALPITOAD*

BATTLE 2

 V

EMOLGA* V PALPITOAD

CASTELIA CITY GYM

BOLT BADGE

BURGH V ASH

This battle against the Bug-type expert is a 3-on-3 battle.

BATTLE 1

 V

DWEBBLE* V TEPIG

BATTLE 2

 V

DWEBBLE V SEWADDLE*

Ash needed eight badges from Unova League gyms before he could enter the Vertress Conference. As had become his habit when going to a new region, Ash left all his Pokémon in the Oak Corral so he could have a fresh start in a new region ... except Pikachu.

*winner
** winner after a match withdrawal
*** forced withdrawal into Poké Ball
**** double KO
***** faints

BATTLE 1

PANSEAR V TEPIG*

BATTLE 2

PANPOUR* V PIKACHU

BATTLE 3

PANSAGE V OSHAWOTT*

BATTLE 2

WATCHOG**** V OSHAWOTT****

BATTLE 3

HERDIER V TEPIG*

Ash planned on Palpitoad taking out the whole team alone on type advantage, so had to run to the Pokémon Centre to get his next Pokémon.

BATTLE 3

EMOLGA* V SNIVY

BATTLE 4

EMOLGA V PIKACHU*

BATTLE 5

TYNAMO V PIKACHU*

BATTLE 3

WHIRLIPEDE V SEWADDLE / SWADLOON*

Sewaddle evolved into Swadloon mid-battle!

BATTLE 4

LEAVANNY* V SWADLOON

BATTLE 5

LEAVANNY V PIKACHU*

DRIFTVEIL CITY GYM

QUAKE BADGE

CLAY V ASH
Ash's first request for a battle was rejected by Clay, until he brought him some Revival Herbs from Milos Island. After gathering the herb, Ash finally got his battle for the badge.

 V

KROKOROK — **OSHAWOTT***

BATTLE 2

 V

PALPITOAD* — **OSHAWOTT**

MISTRALTON CITY GYM

JET BADGE

SKYLA V ASH
When Ash first met Skyla she had lost her motivation to be a gym leader and wanted to become a pilot instead, so she declines Ash's challenge. She later reluctantly accepts, and this battle is a 3-on-3 match.

BATTLE 1

 V

SWOOBAT* — **KROKOROK**

BATTLE 2

 V

SWOOBAT — **TRANQUILL***

ICIRRUS CITY GYM

FREEZE BADGE

BRYCEN V ASH
When Ash entered this gym he slipped over immediately on the ice battlefield. This was a 3-on-3 battle.

BATTLE 1

 V

VANILLISH** — **KROKOROK**

VIRBANK CITY GYM

TOXIC BADGE

ROXIE V ASH
When Ash challenged Roxie he was surprised to learn that he was allowed to use all six of his Pokémon team against her three.

BATTLE 1

 V

KOFFING* — **BOLDORE**

BATTLE 2

 V

KOFFING* — **UNFEZANT**

BATTLE 3

 V

PALPITOAD   SNIVY*

BATTLE 4

 V

EXCADRILL*   SNIVY

BATTLE 5

 V

EXCADRILL   ROGGENROLA / BOLDORE*

Roggenrola evolved into Boldore mid-battle!

BATTLE 3

 V

UNFEZANT   PIKACHU*

BATTLE 4

 V

SWANNA*   PIKACHU

BATTLE 5

 V

SWANNA   TRANQUILL / UNFEZANT*

Tranquill evolved into Unfezant mid-battle!

BATTLE 2

 V

VANILLISH   SCRAGGY*

BATTLE 3

 V

CRYOGONAL*   SCRAGGY

BATTLE 4

 V

CRYOGONAL   PIGNITE*

BATTLE 5

 V

BEARTIC   KROKOROK*

BATTLE 3

KOFFING V LEAVANNY*

BATTLE 4

SCOLIPEDE* V LEAVANNY

BATTLE 5

SCOLIPEDE V PIGNITE*

BATTLE 6

GARBODOR* V PIGNITE

BATTLE 7

GARBODOR V PIKACHU*

VERTRESS CONFERENCE

The Unova League Conference takes place every year in Vertress City. In order to enter, each Trainer must have won eight badges from Unova League gyms.

* winner
** winner after a match withdrawal
*** interrupted battle
**** double KO
***** faints

PRELIMINARY ROUND

128 Trainers enter a 1-on-1 battle, with 64 making it to the next round. Ash's first match is against his rival, Trip.

BATTLE

SERPERIOR V PIKACHU*

After a fierce battle, it looked like Pikachu was about to lose when Serperior got it in a Wrap. Pikachu freed itself using Iron Tail and then it used a combination move of Iron Tail and Electro Ball to defeat Serperior and win the match.

OPENING ROUND

It's a 2-on-2 battle, with the winning 32 Trainers advancing. Ash, Stephan and Virgil all made it to the next round.

BATTLE

DARUMAKA V SCRAGGY*

Scraggy landed a flashy yet graceful High Jump Kick move to send Darumaka flying, and then knocked out Darumaka with Headbutt to advance Ash to the next round.

ROUND 3 Stephan v Ash

The third-round battles are 3-on-3, where Trainers are randomly assigned an opponent. Ash takes on Stephan.

BATTLE 1

LIEPARD V KROOKODILE*

It's Dark type versus Dark type, so the smartest strategy would win. Liepard did Double Team, Krookdile used Dig. Then it was the battle of the claws, with Krookodile taking out Liepard.

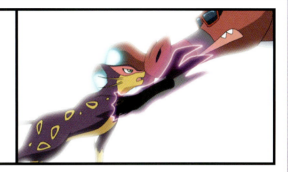

BATTLE 2

ZEBSTRIKA** V PALPITOAD*****

Water- and Ground-type Palpitoad had the advantage here, as Zebstrika's Electric moves had no effect … But Ash hadn't factored in Zebstrika's speed and it managed to dodge many attacks.

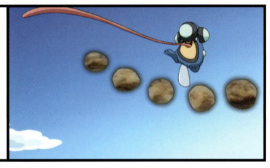

BATTLE 3

SAWK* V LEAVANNY

Down to his last Pokémon, Stephan chose Sawk. Leavanny was able to stop Sawk's Bulk Up with String Shot. Sawk broke the string with X-Scissor, did Karate Chop and knocked Leavanny out.

BATTLE 4

SAWK V KROOKODILE*

Krookodile had a big type disadvantage, as well as being tired from the previous battle, but it was still ready to go! Ash surprised Stephan by having Krookodile perform a new move, Aerial Ace, to win.

QUARTER-FINALS

For the quarter-finals, it's a full 6-on-6 battle and Ash was battling against another of his friends, Cameron.

BATTLE 1
HYDREIGON* V BOLDORE

Boldore was severely weakened after being hit with Tri Attack and Dragon Rush. Boldore's Flash Cannon collided mid-air with Dragon Pulse, before Flash Cannon was overpowered and Boldore got hit and knocked out.

BATTLE 2
HYDREIGON* V OSHAWOTT

Oshawott landed some big hits on the huge Pokémon, with Hydro Pump, Razor Shell and Tackle. Nevertheless, it was no match for Hydreigon.

BATTLE 3
HYDREIGON V PIGNITE*

Pignite started the match hitting Hydreigon with a strong Brick Break. The battle ended with the Pokémon colliding and Hydreigon being defeated.

BATTLE 4
FERROTHORN V PIGNITE*

Pignite was able to dodge Ferrothorn's attacks, Metal Claw and Mirror Shot, but took some damage from Pin Missile. But when Pignite dodged Mirror Charge and used Flame Charge, Ferrothorn was knocked out, giving Pignite its second win.

BATTLE 5
SAMUROTT* V PIGNITE

Pignite was at a type advantage against Water-type Samurott. Despite this, and although it landed some hits on Samurott, it took two huge Water-type attacks from Hydro Cannon and Aqua Jet and was knocked out.

BATTLE 6
SAMUROTT V PIKACHU*

The two Pokémon each landed some huge attacks. Pikachu was hit by Hydro Cannon, but managed to dodge Mega Horn. Ash leaned into the type advantage that his best buddy had for this battle. When Pikachu launched Quick Attack, Ash called for Iron Tail and Electro Ball in quick succession. Samurott managed to block Electro Ball, but was eventuallly knocked out.

BATTLE 7
SWANNA V PIKACHU*

Pikachu and Swanna are both very fast Pokémon and both used their quickest moves to attack and dodge. Pikachu used its Electro Ball move to take the win.

BATTLE 8
RIOLU* V UNFEZANT

When Unfezant did Aerial Ace, Riolu used the momentum to use Circle Throw, and grabbed Unfezant and threw it into the wall, knocking it out.

BATTLE 9
RIOLU / LUCARIO* V SNIVY

Riolu landed a tirade of attacks on Snivy with a Force Palm and Circle Throw combination. Snivy hit the wall but got up again. Snivy managed to land several moves that dealt Riolu a lot of damage. Just as it looked like the end of the battle for Riolu, it stood up and evolved into Lucario! As soon as Lucario demonstrated its new move, Aura Sphere, it was over for Snivy.

Riolu evolved into Lucario mid-battle!

BATTLE 10
LUCARIO* V PIKACHU

Pikachu opened the battle with Quick Attack and managed to dodge Force Palm by jumping over Lucario, but Lucario caught Pikachu and used Circle Throw. Pikachu landed on its feet and did Thunderbolt and Iron Tail, Lucario countered with Copycat and the two attacks collided and created an explosion. Both Pokémon were injured but bravely stood back up. The two Pokémon used Electro Ball and Aura Sphere at the same time, and the attacks collided at first, but then Aura Sphere overpowered Electro Ball and Pikachu took the hit and was knocked out.

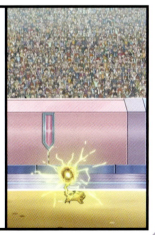

WELCOME TO THE ...
KALOS REGION

The Kalos region is well-known for being shaped like a five-pointed star. It has three main subregions: Central Kalos, covered in forests and rivers, Coastal Kalos, where most of the populated cities and towns are and Mountain Kalos, where the Power Plant, Poké Ball Factory and Pokémon League are located. The largest city in the region, Lumiose City, is in the centre where all three subregions meet.

The Kalos region has the largest Pokédex in the world. It is known as a place of beauty, from its lush forests to sparkling cities and castles. The towns are all named after ingredients used in fragrances.

BADGES ASH WON

In the Kalos region, Pokémon Trainers must earn eight badges from the city gym leaders before they can enter the annual Lumiose Conference.

Gym Leader:
Viola
Santalune City Gym
Type: Bug

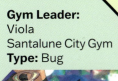

BUG

Gym Leader:
Grant
Cyllage City Gym
Type: Rock

CLIFF

Gym Leader:
Korrina
Shalour City Gym
Type: Fighting

RUMBLE

Gym Leader:
Ramos
Coumarine City Gym
Type: Grass

PLANT

Gym Leader:
Clemont
Lumiose City Gym
Type: Electric

VOLTAGE

Gym Leader:
Valerie
Laverre City Gym
Type: Fairy

FAIRY

Gym Leader:
Olympia
Anistar City Gym
Type: Psychic

PSYCHIC

Gym Leader:
Wulfric
Snowbelle City Gym
Type: Ice

ICEBERG

POKÉMON SKY RELAY

RUNNER-UP

This Sky Relay race consisted of three legs, where the Trainer entered one Pokémon for each leg. The relay went through a forest and a canyon of towering rocks. Ash entered with Fletchinder, Hawlucha and Noibat. Fletchinder was in third place when Hawlucha began the second leg. Hawlucha jumped between the rocks to get some extra speed and launched itself into first place. Noibat started in first place closely followed by Orson's Starly, until a gust of wind took it down. Starly recovered and it was a mad dash to the end, with Noibat losing the race by a beak.

ASH'S CATCHES

A new region means a new, powerful team of Pokémon! In the Kalos region, Ash's team involved his loyal Pikachu and some new friends.

FROAKIE / FROGADIER / GRENINJA

TYPE:
Water / Dark

As a first partner Pokémon, Froakie would often abandon its new Trainers and return to the lab. It is stubborn and picky, but deeply loyal and protective to Ash and his friends. It is strongest in its Ash-Greninja form.

Read more about Greninja's Ash-Greninja form on page 152.

FLETCHLING / FLETCHINDER / TALONFLAME

TYPE:
Fire / Flying

As a Fletchling, it lost to Ash's Froakie and was captured, but it was humble in defeat and shared a berry with Pikachu and Froakie to show friendship. Fletchinder won an Honor of Kalos medal for fighting against Team Flare.

HAWLUCHA

TYPE:
Fighting / Flying

Hawlucha's biggest achievement in battle was winning against Astrid's Mega-Evolved Absol, despite not being Mega-Evolved itself. Hawlucha prefers speedy moves, and always finishes its opponents with a Flying Press.

SLIGGOO / GOODRA

TYPE:
Dragon

It is a very friendly Pokémon, and it likes to show its affection to others by nibbling on their ears. Sliggoo used Rain Dance to protect Ash from a fire, which led to its Evolution to Goodra. This same move activated its Hydration ability.

NOIBAT / NOIVERN

TYPE:
Flying / Dragon

Noibat is particularly close with Hawlucha, who takes it under its wing after it hatches, and teaches it how to fly. Noivern has battled several powerful opponents, including Zapdos, Salamence and Lysandre's Shiny Gyarados.

PROFESSOR SYCAMORE

Professor Augustine Sycamore is the professor in the Kalos region. He is kind and goes out of his way to be helpful to people when they need it, and always remains calm.

Sycamore can often be found travelling around the region to attend Pokémon showcases, conducting his research and running a Summer Camp that Ash and his friends attend. New Trainers in the Kalos region go to Professor Sycamore's lab in Lumiose City and can choose between the three first partners for the region: Chespin, Fennekin and Froakie.

Sycamore has a devoted Garchomp constantly at his side. The two first met when Garchomp was a Gible. Sycamore's research and speciality is Mega Evolution, and his bond with Garchomp helped it achieve transformation into Mega Garchomp.

GARCHOMP

HOW SYCAMORE MET ASH

When Team Rocket attacked Ash and Clemont in the middle of their battle, a Froakie appeared and helped them fight. It protected Pikachu and got injured. Ash rushed it back to Sycamore's lab so it could be healed. Later, when Team Rocket put a pain collar on Garchomp and it went on a rampage, Ash climbed to the top of Prism Tower to help it. From this moment, Ash and Sycamore became good friends. Sycamore saw that Froakie, after rejecting many of its past Trainers, had bonded with Ash and he gave his approval for the pair to form a legendary match.

CLEMONT

Clemont is the Lumiose City Gym leader and an Electric-type expert, but is better known for his inventions. There's nothing Clemont likes more than solving a problem with a gadget.

Clemont attended a prestigious school that focused on Electric-type Pokémon. He once found an exhausted Shinx and when he rushed it to the Pokémon Centre, Nurse Joy told him that she believed that something in the environment was draining the Electric-type Pokémon. Clemont was determined to help and invented a special recharging chamber that rains electricity. This invention remains in the city for all Electric-type Pokémon to use.

HOW CLEMONT MET ASH

When Ash first arrived in the Kalos region, he ran straight to challenge the Lumiose Gym. But instead of a challenge, Ash came face to face with Clembot, who zapped him out of the gym. Luckily Clemont was outside and caught him on a giant inflatable pillow.

After Clemont saw Ash's brave rescue of Professor Sycamore's Garchomp, he decided to travel with Ash so he could learn more.

Bonnie is Clemont's younger sister. She is too young to be a Pokémon Trainer, but that doesn't stop her from wanting to be around them all the time! She begged Clemont to catch Dedenne so that she could take care of it. Since then, Dedenne has stayed at Bonnie's side, often out of its Poké Ball inside of Bonnie's backpack. The only thing she loves more than cute Pokémon is her big brother – she is very proud of him and all of his inventions.

HOW BONNIE MET ASH

Bonnie met Ash at the same time that Clemont did. As Clemont's inflatable pillow caught Ash, Bonnie caught Pikachu and was so excited, she gave it a huge hug … and Pikachu gave her a shock!

Serena is the daughter of the famous Rhyhorn racer, Grace. Serena wanted to live up to her mother's legacy, but the only problem was that she hated riding Rhyhorns! She wasn't sure what she wanted to do until she turned on the TV one day and saw her old friend, Ash. She knew she had to find him!

Serena got her first Pokémon from Professor Sycamore and chose a Fennekin. Serena has lots of style and she loves to express her love for her Pokémon by dressing them up as well. It helps her and her Pokémon feel confident. After travelling with Ash for a while, she realised that her dream was to become a Pokémon performer. She has won three Princess Keys – Dendemille, Anistar and Fleurrh.

HOW SERENA MET ASH

When Serena attended Professor Oak's Summer Camp, she was out in the woods and was startled by a Poliwag, and she fell and hurt her knee. Ash stopped to help her and wrapped her knee in his handkerchief. He then helped her out of the forest. When Serena went to meet Ash in the Kalos region she brought the handkerchief so that he would remember.

TRAINER TIPS: ASH AND GRENINJA

Ash's first catch in the Kalos region was very special. Its evolved form, Greninja, became one of Ash's most powerful battlers and his only Pokémon to activate the Bond Phenomenon.

THE KALOS REGION

THE LEGEND OF THE NINJA HERO

Ash was with his Frogadier in the Kalos region forest, when his old friend, Sanpei, emerged with his Greninja. He took Ash to his home, Ninja Village. Long ago, the village was a chaotic place where two groups of ninjas were constantly battling. The Pokémon of the village grouped together to defend it from the ninjas, with a Greninja as the leader.

Deep under the village, there was a monument built to honour the Greninja, the ninja hero, which told the tale of the battles. Sanpei and his brother, Ippei, had both chosen Froakie as their first partner Pokémon to honour this hero.

When a flock of Skarmony attacked Ninja Village and the alarm was sounded, it was discovered that the village was under siege by a ninja called Kagetomo and his Ninja Corps, who kidnapped the chief, Hanzo.

Kagetomo used to live in Ninja Village. He was very powerful and destined to become the next chief, until he had an argument with Hanzo. 'To continue to train along with and discover the possibilities of Pokémon to defend the people of the world. That and that alone, is the role of the ninja,' Hanzo told him. But Kagetomo wanted to use his powers to rule the world, and so he left and started the Ninja Corps for revenge.

Ash and his friends bravely volunteered to help rescue Hanzo from the Ninja Corps. Ash and Sanpei battled against Heidayu and his Bisharp

but their combined attacks from Greninja, Ash's Frogadier and Pikachu were having little effect. When Bisharp was about to attack an injured Pikachu with Shadow Claw, Frogadier stepped in front to protect it and evolved into Greninja!

It was during this intense battle with Bisharp that something awesome happened; Ash's Greninja changed into a special form, unlocking the Bond Phenomenon for the first time! It was connected to its Trainer like never before, and the pair became unstoppable, defeating Bisharp with ease.

'What did Greninja just do?' Ash wondered in confusion and awe of Greninja's power.

After helping to save Ninja Village, Ash and his friends left to continue their adventures. Sanpei told Ippei and Hanzo what happened with Ash and his Greninja and how it changed its appearance during battle. All were convinced that Ash's Greninja has proven itself to be the successor of the ancient ninja hero, who had returned to protect the village once again.

BOND PHENOMENON

What exactly is the Bond Phenomenon that Ash and Greninja tapped into? It is a Mega Evolution-type transformation that occurs when the bond between a Pokémon and Trainer is at its maximum. It doesn't require a stone, and not every Pokémon can achieve it. In fact, it is so rare that Ash's Greninja is the first known Pokémon to be able to do this in over 300 years, since the Hero-Greninja from Ninja Village.

While the Pokémon and Trainer are using this form, the Trainer shares the Pokémon's pain and can see its point of view. Even though Ash and Greninja could often tap into the power by accident, it was something they had to work hard at and train together to master. Clemont's Synchronicity Test device, which measured how synchronised Ash and Greninja were in battle, helped the two of them learn to activate their Ash-Greninja form on command.

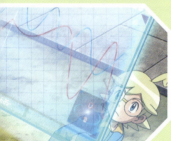

A LOSS OF CONFIDENCE

While they were still learning, Ash and Greninja lost a few tough battles. When they faced Sawyer and his Grovyle, Ash began to overthink his opponent's next move, which distracted him. He and Greninja failed to activate Bond Phenomenon in that moment, which caused them to lose the battle. Not long afterwards, in a further knock to Ash's confidence, they lost in the battle for their eighth Gym Badge against an Avalugg.

Ash lost all his confidence and felt unworthy of being Greninja's Trainer; he wondered if he would even be able to bring out its true powers. Ash went for a walk in the snow-covered forest, looking for answers. Greninja, in sync with Ash as always, followed him. A huge snowstorm whipped up in the forest and in that moment, Greninja knew it needed to get to Ash to help him.

Meanwhile, Ash was trying to rescue as many Pokémon as he could to shelter them from the storm in a cave. Ash spotted a Spewpa shivering on a branch and headed out of the cave to rescue it, but in the chaos of the storm, he and the Spewpa ended up falling down a ravine. At the last second, Greninja appeared as if from nowhere and rescued them using its long tongue … but the Spewpa slipped out of Ash's arms and back into the ravine!

Greninja knew the only way it could save the Spewpa was by using the extra speed Bond Phenomenon gave it. Without hesitation, it jumped and activated its special form. Ash-Greninja swooped down after the Spewpa, caught it, then used its shared sight with Ash to safely jump between branches and rocks to land on the ground. After saving the Spewpa, the pair sheltered in the cave until the storm ended, and Ash shared stories of his youth. He realised that he and Greninja were partners and they should always work together. Greninja offered Ash a Poké Ball, to remind his Trainer of their friendship.

THE PERFECT PAIRING

Professor Sycamore showed Ash an old manuscript, which told him all about the Bond Phenomenon, and how the Pokémon has to have a special ability to activate this in the first place. He believed that this Greninja's earlier form, Froakie, had chosen Ash back in the lab, knowing he could bring out its true powers. It had rejected so many other Trainers until it met Ash and snuck away to join his team.

TRAINER TALES

There are lots of adventures to be had in the Kalos region. Here, Ash learns about Mega Evolution and fights Mega-Evolved Pokémon in battles.

1 PROFESSOR SYCAMORE'S SUMMER CAMP

At this week-long camp, Ash and his friends were put into Team Froakie – were they able to work together, win the most points and secure a place in the Summer Camp Hall of Fame?

POKÉMON BATTLE TOURNAMENT
This was a battle where the first Pokémon to touch the other won. The idea was that everyone could get to know each other. It was Serena's first-ever official battle with Fennekin, against Shauna and Bulbasaur. Ash and Froakie lost to Tierno and his dancing Squirtle.

FISHING COMPETITION
On day two of the camp, the teams competed in a fishing competition, where the biggest catch was the winner! Ash caught an Alomomola. Serena caught a Staryu. Clemont caught a Corphish. It was victory for Team Squirtle, with Team Froakie tied for third place.

POKÉVISION COMPETITION
Day three's competition was to make Pokévision videos, which would be shown at the end of the day and voted on by the other teams. Team Froakie filmed a video in a flower field about Serena's Poké Puffs – and these looked so delicious that they came in first place!

POKÉENTEERING COMPETITION
On the fifth day, the teams competed to collect stamps from seven checkpoints and the first team back to the camp would win. Team Froakie were leading until Bonnie became lost in the foggy forest. Bonnie had spotted an unknown Pokémon and followed it so the rest of the team had to stop racing to go to find her. Team Froakie was so late back that they didn't earn any points.

TEAM BATTLE TOURNAMENT
On the last day of camp, the teams competed in a battle, with three Trainers on each side. The final came down to Team Froakie versus Team Squirtle. The teams were on equal points going into the final day, so this battle was the decider. It was a close call, but Team Froakie took the win!

2 PIKACHU V MEGA LUCARIO

Korrina, the leader of Shalour City Gym, is a descendant of the first people who managed to make a Lucario reach Mega Evolution. The leader of Shalour City Gym had a tradition of being partnered with a Mega-Evolved Lucario.

When they first met, Korrina and Lucario wanted to train together and win 100 battles before they got a Mega Stone. Her grandfather had told Korrina the bond of trust between Trainer and Pokémon was just as important for Mega Evolution as the stone.

Their 99th battle was against Ash and Pikachu, who had no answer to Lucario's powerful Bone Rush attack. Their 100th battle win was a tag-team battle with Ash and Pikachu against Team Rocket. After this, they all travelled to Geosenge Town so Korrina could get the Lucarionite Mega Stone.

After the team helped Korrina through the Cave of Trials to find Lucarionite, Lucario finally Mega-Evolved and an excited Ash challenged them on the spot! Mega Lucario's power was off the charts, but it was unable to control itself, flying into a red-eyed rage, viciously attacking Pikachu and refusing to listen to Korrina. It could only be stopped when her grandfather's Lucario stepped in and knocked it out of its Mega Evolution.

Korrina was devastated, but Ash reassured her that she and Lucario would work out how to control its new powers together. Her grandfather sent them both to train further at Pomace Mountain to understand Mega Evolution.

The gang headed to the top of the mountain to visit and train with Mabel and her Mega-Evolved Mawile. Mabel told Korrina that though she and Lucario understood each other deeply, they had two viewpoints and needed to bring those together to master Mega Evolution.

After parting ways, Ash and Korrina agreed to train separately for a while and then meet up again for their gym battle. The battle came down to Mega Lucario versus Pikachu. It was an epic and powerful battle that ended when Aura Sphere collided with Electro Ball and exploded in the air. Before Mega Lucario was able to move, Pikachu defeated it with Thunderbolt.

BATTLE BREAKDOWN

THE KALOS REGION GYM

SANTALUNE CITY GYM

BUG BADGE

VIOLA V ASH

In his first attempt at the Bug Badge, Ash lost when Surskit used Ice Beam to freeze the battlefield. After some practise, Ash was ready to challenge Viola again.

BATTLE 1

SURSKIT

V

PIKACHU*

CYLLAGE CITY GYM

CLIFF BADGE

GRANT V ASH

Ash had to climb a rock face to make it to the battlefield in the first place. Grant isn't allowed any substitutions, but Ash can use as many Pokémon as he has.

BATTLE 1

ONIX

V

FROAKIE*

SHALOUR CITY GYM

RUMBLE BADGE

KORRINA V ASH

For this match, Ash tried to use the rhythmic battle style he had learned from Tierno, but this didn't go well. Serena reminded him to use his own style.

BATTLE 1

MIENFOO

V

HAWLUCHA*

COUMARINE CITY GYM

PLANT BADGE

RAMOS V ASH

Ash first met Ramos and his Gogoat when they helped him save a Vanillish and Vanilluxe from Team Rocket. This was a 3-on-3 battle.

BATTLE 1

JUMPLUFF

V

FLETCHINDER*

BATTLE 2

WEEPINBELL*

V

FLETCHINDER

Ash required eight badges from Kalos League gyms before he could enter the Lumiose Conference. He needed to come up with new strategies to defeat his opponents but always rely on his instincts.

* winner
** winner after a match withdrawal
*** forced withdrawal into Poké Ball
**** double KO
***** faints

BATTLE 2

VIVILLON* V FLETCHLING

BATTLE 3

VIVILLON V PIKACHU*

BATTLE 2

TYRUNT* V FROAKIE

BATTLE 3

TYRUNT* V FLETCHLING

BATTLE 4

TYRUNT V PIKACHU*

BATTLE 2

MACHOKE* V FLETCHINDER

BATTLE 3

LUCARIO (MEGA-EVOLVED)* V FLETCHINDER

BATTLE 4

LUCARIO (MEGA-EVOLVED) V PIKACHU*

BATTLE 3

WEEPINBELL* V HAWLUCHA

BATTLE 4

WEEPINBELL V FROGADIER*

BATTLE 5

GOGOAT V FROGADIER*

159

LUMIOSE CITY GYM

VOLTAGE BADGE

CLEMONT V ASH
After travelling together around the Kalos region, Ash finally gets to challenge Clemont for an official Voltage Badge. This was a 3-on-3 battle.

BATTLE 1

 **BUNNELBY** V  **PIKACHU***

BATTLE 2

 **HELIOLISK**** V  **GOODRA**

LAVERRE CITY GYM

FAIRY BADGE

VALERIE V ASH
As well as being a gym leader, Valerie is also a famous fashion designer. She arrived on the battlefield in a cloud of flower petals for the 2-on-2 battle.

BATTLE 1

 **SYLVEON** V  **FLETCHINDER***

ANISTAR CITY GYM

PSYCHIC BADGE

OLYMPIA V ASH
This gym showdown is a Double Battle. Olympia's team of Meowstic and their combination of Helping Hand and Future Sight seemed unbeatable at first. Ash finally saw what was going on and coached his Pokémon to victory.

BATTLE

 **MEOWSTIC AND MEOWSTIC** V  **TALONFLAME AND FROGADIER***

SNOWBELLE CITY GYM

ICEBERG BADGE

WULFRIC V ASH
Ash lost his first challenge for the Iceberg Badge, despite using more Pokémon than Wulfric. Wulfric didn't think Ash had enough trust in his Greninja so they went away and perfected their partnership.

BATTLE 1

 **BERGMITE** V  **PIKACHU***

BATTLE 3

 v

HELIOLISK | **HAWLUCHA***

BATTLE 4

 v

LUXRAY* | **HAWLUCHA**

BATTLE 5

 v

LUXRAY* | **PIKACHU**

BATTLE 6

 v

LUXRAY | **GOODRA***

BATTLE 2

SPRITZEE* | **FLETCHINDER**

BATTLE 3

SPRITZEE | **HAWLUCHA***

BATTLE 2

 v

AVALUGG* | **PIKACHU**

BATTLE 3

 v

AVALUGG | **TALONFLAME***

BATTLE 4

 v

ABOMASNOW* | **TALONFLAME**

BATTLE 5

 v

ABOMASNOW | **ASH-GRENINJA***

LUMIOSE CONFERENCE

The Lumiose Conference is held annually and uses themed battlefields, such as Forest and Badlands, as well as the more traditional Rock, Ice, Grass and Water.

* winner
** winner after a match withdrawal
*** forced withdrawal into Poké Ball
**** double KO
***** faints

PRELIMINARIES Titus v Ash

In the first rounds, 64 Trainers are reduced to 32. Then the second, only eight competitors advance to the quarter-finals.

BATTLE

ALTARIA V GRENINJA*

Ash was late to his battle with Titus after being intercepted by an old rival outside the stadium. He sent Greninja in to fight Altaria, and once it activated the Bond Phenomenon, it was an easy victory.

QUARTER-FINALS Astrid v Ash

At the end of the quarter-finals, only four competitors remain. These are 3-on-3 battles, with match-ups decided randomly.

BATTLE

MEGA ABSOL V HAWLUCHA*

Astrid commanded her Mega Absol to use Psycho Cut against Ash's Hawlucha, but it dodged the attack. It then landed a direct knock-out hit with Flying Press, securing Ash's place in the semi-finals.

SEMI-FINALS Sawyer v Ash

The semi-finals are full 6-on-6 battles with a break between bouts while the battlefield is changed.

BATTLE 1 — SLAKING* V HAWLUCHA

Hawlucha did several moves but they had little effect; Slaking didn't even flinch! Slaking used Counter to knock Hawlucha out.

BATTLE 2 — SLAKING V TALONFLAME*

Ash was confident that the damage Hawlucha inflicted in the first battle would give Talonflame the upper hand. It used Brave Bird to win.

BATTLE 3 — CLAWITZER* V TALONFLAME

Sawyer had successfully trained Clawitzer to use Aqua Jet to fly through the air, a strategy he learned from Ash.

BATTLE 4 — CLAWITZER V PIKACHU*

Pikachu used its speed and agility to jump between the trees in the forest to its advantage. A Thunderbolt handed Ash the win.

BATTLE 5 — AEGISLASH V PIKACHU*

Aegislash started by cutting all the trees down to litter the field and slow Pikachu down. It was unsuccessful and Pikachu prevailed.

BATTLEFIELD CHANGE: Badlands

BATTLE 6 — SALAMENCE**** V NOIVERN****

The pair exchanged fierce aerial attacks, but their moves collided powerfully and knocked them both out.

BATTLE 7 — SLURPUFF**** V GOODRA****

Goodra used Bide as Slurpuff did Fairy Wind and, as the smoke cleared from the attacks' collision, it revealed a double knock-out, again!

BATTLE 8 — SCEPTILE* V PIKACHU

Pikachu was still tired from his double win earlier in the competition, so was no match for Sceptile's Frenzy Plant attack.

BATTLE 9 — MEGA SCEPTILE V ASH-GRENINJA*

Mega Sceptile was powerful, but Ash and Greninja became more synchronised throughout the battle, winning Ash a place in the final!

FINALS Alain v Ash

As in the semi-finals, the grand final has a break for the battlefield changeover. Ash takes on Alain.

BATTLE 1 — TYRANITAR V PIKACHU*

Even though Tyranitar activated its Sand Stream ability to make it difficult for Pikachu to see, it didn't succeed. When Tyranitar caught Pikachu's Iron Tail in its mouth, Pikachu did a close-range Electro Ball, which knocked it out.

BATTLE 2 — WEAVILE* V NOIVERN

When Weavile's Ice Beam clipped and froze part of Noivern's wing, it fell into the water. Weavile then hit the water with Night Slash, which secured the win.

BATTLE 3 — WEAVILE V HAWLUCHA*

After Weavile froze the water, Hawlucha was able to use the ice to reduce any damage. Hawlucha got stronger with every attack then knocked Weavile out with Flying Press.

BATTLE 4 — BISHARP* V HAWLUCHA

Although Hawlucha was tired from the previous battle, it still managed to withstand Thunder Wave and land X-Scissor. After a collision and a failed High Jump Kick, Bisharp used Guillotine and knocked Hawlucha out.

BATTLE 5 — UNFEZANT**** V TALONFLAME****

After both Pokémon exhibited their flying prowess, they attacked each other simultaneously, with Sky Attack from Unfezant and Brave Bird from Talonflame, and the head-on collision knocked both out.

BATTLEFIELD CHANGE: Grass

BATTLE 6 — METAGROSS V PIKACHU*

Pikachu took huge hits from Metagross, but it still managed to stand up and counter Meteor Mash with Electro Ball. Pikachu then managed to jump on top of Metagross and delivered a Thundershock which did critical damage. Metagross managed to shake Pikachu off, but it came back quickly with Iron Tail and knocked Metagross out.

BATTLE 7 — CHARIZARD* V PIKACHU

Pikachu opened strongly but was tired from the previous battle. It got hit by Charizard's Flame Thrower. Pikachu battled on but was eventually defeated.

BATTLE 8 — BISHARP* V GOODRA

Ash had Goodra do Rain Dance to make a favourable environment for it to battle. But the powerful Goodra was no match for Bisharp's speed and Iron Head attack.

BATTLE 9 — BISHARP V GRENINJA*

With Rain Dance still in effect, Greninja's Water-type moves were powered-up. Bisharp charged at Greninja who did Double Team to focus it, then Greninja jumped up and knocked Bisharp out with Water Shuriken.

BATTLE 10 — MEGA CHARIZARD* V ASH-GRENINJA

The two Pokémon exchanged some powerful moves. Mega Charizard used its most impressive attack, Blast Burn, but Ash-Greninja countered by slamming its Water Shuriken into the ground like a pick-axe to block the move. Using the steam as a cover, Ash-Greninja got close enough to Mega Charizard to use Aerial Ace and knock it to the ground. Mega Charizard countered with Blast Burn and the attacks collided, causing a huge explosion, which knocked Charizard out of its Mega Evolution and Greninja from the Bond Phenomenon. Both stumbled but Greninja fainted first, giving Alain the win.

WELCOME TO THE ...
ALOLA REGION

The Alola region is made up of five islands. Four of the islands are natural – Melemele Island, Akala Island, Ula'ula Island and Poni Island – and the final one is the artificial island, Aether Paradise. There are nine towns and cities with the largest city of Hau'oli on Melemele Island. This island has a mountain, and the Ruins of Conflict are at the top.

Akala Island contains the region's only active volcano, Wela Volcano. Ula'ula is the largest island, which has the most variable weather and roughest terrain. Each natural island has its own Guardian: Melemele – Tapu Koko, Akala – Tapu Lele, Ula'ula – Tapu Bulu, Poni – Tapu Fini. In the Alola region, humans and Pokémon coexist together and they have developed a close relationship – the culture overall is different than other regions. To say 'hello' and 'goodbye', you say 'Alola'!

The Alola region's environment affects the Pokémon in various ways and creates distinct Alolan variants. For instance, the Alolan Exeggutor is five times taller than other regions due to the abundance of sunlight in the Alola region. The Alolan Vulpix moved to the snowy mountains to avoid the habitats of other Pokémon and adapted by becoming white and an Ice type.

Z-CRYSTALS

In the Alola region, things work a little differently than in the other regions. Instead of collecting badges through gym battles, Trainers compete in challenges to collect Z-Crystals, which are then stored in Z-Rings, and used to perform Z-Moves.

Ash decided to take on the Alolan Island Challenge of obtaining Z-Crystals by travelling around the islands and defeating various Totem Pokémon and Grand Trials.

ELECTRIUM Z
Received from Tapu Koko

MELEMELE ISLAND GRAND TRIAL

NORMALIUM Z
Received from Totem Gumshoos

VERDANT CAVERN TRIAL

GRASSIUM Z
Received from Totem Lurantis

LUSH JUNGLE TRIAL

ROCKIUM Z
Received from Kahuna Olivia

AKALA ISLAND GRAND TRIAL

PIKASHUNIUM Z
Transformed from Electrium Z

THRIFTY MEGAMART TRIAL

LYCANIUM Z
Received from Kahuna Nanu

ULA'ULA ISLAND GRAND TRIAL

STEELIUM Z
Received from Kahuna Hapu

PONI ISLAND GRAND TRIAL

POKÉMON SLED JUMP GAMES!

When Ash and his friends arrived on the island of Ula'ula, they discovered an annual bobsled competition was happening on the region's tallest mountain, Mount Lanakila. The lure of competition was too strong, so Ash signed up! The Trainer and Pokémon must travel down a ski jump on a PokéSled. Once in the air, the Pokémon must perform at least one move to impress the judges and hopefully increase the distance of the jump overall. Ash and Pikachu attempt to perform a Z-Move Thunder Shock while in the air, but this backfires and propels the pair backwards!

ASH'S CATCHES

Ash started his journey in the Alola region with only Pikachu in his team. He wanted to catch and get to know the new Pokémon in the region.

ROWLET

TYPE: Grass / Flying

Rowlet was born and raised by a flock of Pikipek. It can fly silently and loves to roost inside Ash's backpack. Rowlet was unable to evolve using the Everstone, but instead used it as a weapon to utilise its Z-Moves.

ROCKRUFF / LYCANROC

TYPE: Rock

Lycanroc won Ash his first Pokémon League at the Manalo Conference. Lycanroc is very proud of its fur and can fly into a red-eyed rage when it is threatened. It can harness this rage in battle by remembering a playful memory with Ash.

LITTEN / TORRACAT / INCINEROAR

TYPE: Fire / Dark

Originally Litten liked to be alone, but eventually learned to love Ash and his Pokémon. When Torracat went up against Professor Kukui's Incineroar, it defeated its evolved form using Revenge and then promptly evolved itself.

POIPOLE / NAGANADEL

TYPE: Poison / Dragon

Naganadel is an extra-dimensional Pokémon or Ultra Beast. It joined Ash as a Poipole before evolving. It is a playful trickster and affectionate. It can be dazzled by lights and often stops to admire Pikachu's Electric-type moves.

MELTAN / MELMETAL

TYPE: Steel

Meltan stowed away in Ash's backpack. Later, Melmetal unknowingly ate Ash's badge from Ryuki! Melmetal is Ash's heaviest and his first Mythical Pokémon. Melmetal smashes Gladion's Silvally and Professor Kukui's Empoleon.

Z-MOVES

One of the coolest things about being a Pokémon Trainer in the Alola region is the opportunity to learn Z-Moves. To perform a Z-Move, a Trainer first needs to get a Z-Ring. Ash gets his ring from the Legendary Guardian, Tapu Koko.

The Trainer then needs to compete in the Island Challenges to be awarded with Z-Crystals. To do a Z-Move, the Z-Crystal must be put into the Z-Ring and must match the Pokémon's type. The Trainer also needs to perform specific movements to activate it. Kiawe told Ash that only when a Trainer and their Pokémon's hearts become one will the Z-Ring turn their feelings into power – and those feelings must be about something greater than themselves. Only those who are committed to helping the world are allowed to use Z-Moves.

Z-Moves drain a lot of the Pokémon's energy, but with lots of training, the Pokémon can reduce the amount of energy needed to perform the Z-Move. Z-Moves are much more powerful than regular moves and have a large blast radius, which means they can take out more than one opponent at once.

Z-MOVES ASH USED

NORMALIUM Z
Breakneck Blitz with Pikachu, Rowlet, Rockruff and Litten

ELECTRIUM Z
Gigavolt Havoc with Pikachu – this was the first Z-Move Ash and Pikachu used against Tapu Koko

PIKASHUNIUM Z
10,000,000 Volt Thunderbolt – this is an exclusive move for Pikachu and an upgraded version of Thunderbolt. Pikachu wears Ash's Alolan cap to do this move

GRASSIUM Z
Bloom Doom with Rowlet creating a green aura

ROCKIUM Z
Continental Crush with Lycanroc

LYCANIUM Z
Splintered Stormshards with Lycanroc – this is an exclusive move for Lycanroc and an upgraded version of Stone Edge

STEELIUM Z
Corkscrew Crash with Pikachu

FIRIUM Z
Inferno Overdrive with Torracat – Ash borrowed this Z-Crystal from Professor Kukui

SOLGANIUM Z
Searing Sunraze Smash with Nebby (Solgaleo)

POKÉMON SCHOOL

Ash's holiday to the Alola region with his mum turned into an unexpected adventure, when Delia enrolled him in Pokémon School! Pokémon School is a place where humans and Pokémon all study and learn together and is located on Melemele Island.

Professor Kukui makes sure that every day is full of interesting things for his students to learn and do. The students spend very little time sat studying textbooks, and are instead often out and about, completing challenges and learning about themselves and the world around them.

ANNUAL PANCAKE RACE

The competition is a relay race that involves Trainers and one of their Pokémon carrying a plate stacked with several Alolan pancakes around a course on Melemele Island. If a pancake is dropped, then the competitor is disqualified. Ash came in joint second with Nina, with the overall winner being Professor Samson Oak!

WELA FIRE FESTIVAL

On a class trip to Wela Volcano Park, a rogue Marowak stole the Wela Crown during the Crowning Ceremony. Kiawe ran after it to get it back. The battle between Marowak and Turtonator ended in defeat for Kiawe, after he decided to try and finish the battle quickly by using Z-Move Inferno Overdrive.

Kiawe was frustrated at himself for not being able to get his crown back, but Ash told him they could work together and train to devise a way to beat Marowak. When Kiawe faced Marowak again the next day, he used a new move, Shell Smash, which helped him become stronger and faster. They still lost but Marowak agreed to join Kiawe's team.

FACT FILE

PROFESSOR SAMSON OAK

Professor Samson Oak is the principal of the Pokémon School. Professor Oak from the Kanto region is his cousin, though the two don't meet until the Pokémon School class go on a field trip to Pallet Town.

Samson is a cheerful and excitable person, who loves to make puns using the names of Pokémon, which is usually paired with a visual impression of the Pokémon – this often makes those around him confused!

Ash and his mum first meet Professor Samson while on a mission to deliver an egg for their own Professor Oak.

Professor Samson entered into the Manalo Conference. He battled Hau in the first round, putting his Alolan Exeggutor against the Alolan Raichu, but unfortunately, he was knocked out of the competition.

PROFESSOR KUKUI

Professor Kukui is the professor for the Alola region and a teacher at the Alolan Pokémon School. He studies Pokémon moves and he loves to add moves into his conversations.

Kukui is very serious and calm, but also very cheerful and welcoming, especially to his students. He is married to Professor Burnet and their wedding was set up by the students of the Pokémon School. They have a child together called Lei.

Ash and Kukui have a very close relationship. In fact, Ash lived with him and his family while he was attending the school. Kukui gives Ash his Alolan Pokédex, which is later inhabited by a Rotom.

He lives a secret double life … he is the Masked Royal, a Pokémon wrestler who specialises in Battle Royale. The Masked Royal's partner in battle is Incineroar. The Alolan tradition has four Pokémon enter a ring at once and they battle until the final Pokémon is standing.

ASH'S ALOLAN CLASSMATES

Ash is so excited to learn more about Pokémon and the Alola region as well as make lots of new friends. These are the friends he meets at Pokémon School.

KIAWE

Kiawe attends school while helping at his family's farm, and he delivers packages throughout the region on his Charizard. He is an experienced Trainer and is skilled at Z-Moves. He has a particular love of Fire-type Pokémon.

LILLIE

Lillie is afraid of being touched by Pokémon, although she loves to study them in books. Her fear began when she visited the Aether Paradise and was attacked by an Ultra Beast. Lillie is very knowledgeable and cares deeply for others.

SOPHOCLES

Sophocles met Ash when he first came to Pokémon School. He loves to invent helpful machines. He has a love of Electric-type Pokémon and often uses them to power devices. His dream is to become an astronaut.

LANA

Lana is a lover of the sea and Water-type Pokémon. She is highly protective of Pokémon, especially if she sees someone being cruel to one. Her main aim is to make Pokémon and others happy and will go to great lengths to do so.

MALLOW

Mallow is always in a hurry, so she often misses things! She lives with her family in their restaurant, where all the gang love to hang out. She is friendly and loves to cook food for people. She is particularly keen on Grass-type Pokémon.

ALOLAN ISLAND TRIALS

The Island Challenge was created to teach Trainers to love and protect the islands of the Alola region as well as the people and Pokémon who inhabit them. The final trial on each island is called the Grand Trial. This consists of a series of trials leading up to the final challenge, where the competitor has to face the island Kahuna in battle.

Each trial requires the competitor to defeat a Totem Pokémon, a type of variant Pokémon trained by the trial captain. The challenge is another way for Trainers to earn Z-Crystals, but it is very rare for a Totem Pokémon to gift a Z-Crystal to a challenger.

VERDANT CAVERN TRIAL

Melemele Island had a problem with the Rattata and Raticate eating all the island's food, so Hala, the island Kahuna, asked Ash to help. He led Ash to the Verdant Cavern, where a very strong group of Yungoos and Gumshoos were living. Ash realised he had to challenge the Totem Pokémon to complete the trial. He called out Pikachu and Rowlet to begin the battle.

Totem Gumshoos
Awarded: Normalium Z

BATTLE 1

ROWLET AND PIKACHU* V YUNGOOS AND GUMSHOOS

BATTLE 2

ROWLET AND PIKACHU* V TOTEM GUMSHOOS

Rowlet dived to shield Pikachu from an attack and was knocked out. Ash's strategy was for Pikachu to use Agility to make a dust cloud around Gumshoos so it couldn't see, then use Quick Attack. Finally, Pikachu used Thunderbolt to finish the battle. Ash gained Gumshoos's respect and the Totem agreed to help with the troublesome Rattata and Raticate, and Ash received a Z-Crystal.

* winner

MELEMELE ISLAND GRAND TRIAL

Kahuna Hala v Ash

Received: Electrium Z (Hala originally awarded Fightium Z to Ash, but Tapu Koko switched it for Electrium Z)

BATTLE 1

CRABRAWLER V ROWLET*

BATTLE 2

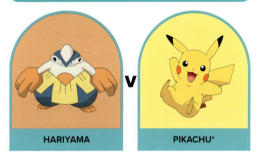

HARIYAMA V PIKACHU*

Ash and Pikachu used Normalium Z to do Breakneck Blitz to win.

LUSH JUNGLE TRIAL

Totem Lurantis
Awarded: Grassium Z

Ash and Mallow were in search of ingredients for the Akala Curry. After finding the Mago Berry and the Revival Herb, they found the final ingredient, Miracle Seed, in a hollowed-out trunk in a cave. Before they could pick it, they were challenged by Totem Lurantis and Castform.

BATTLE 1

LITTEN AND ROWLET*

V

TOTEM LURANTIS AND CASTFORM (SUNNY DAY FORM)

Litten did Breakneck Blitz to win – the second Z-Move Ash had used in battle.

AKALA ISLAND GRAND TRIAL

Kahuna Olivia v Ash
Received: Rockium Z

BATTLE 1

PROBOPASS AND LYCANROC

V

ROCKRUFF AND ROWLET*

Olivia used Continental Crush but Rowlet grabbed Rockruff and flew to evade it. Ash and Rowlet used Grassium-Z to do Bloom Doom to knock out Probopass. Rockruff used Bite on Rowlet to knock it out.

THRIFTY MEGAMART TRIAL

After losing his first challenge to Kahuna Nanu when Lycanroc went into a red-eyed rage, Ash wanted a rematch. Nanu would only agree if Ash won a battle against Team Rocket at the abandoned Thifty Megamart first!

BATTLE 1

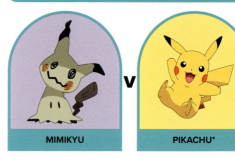

MIMIKYU

V

PIKACHU*

Jessie and Mimikyu used Mimikyu Z to do Let's Snuggle Forever, where it draped its costume over Pikachu. Team Rocket think they have finally caught the Electric type, but Pikachu protected itself using a new move, Electro Web. Ash and Pikachu then use Pikashunium Z to do 10,000,000 Volt Thunderbolt to win.

ULA'ULA ISLAND GRAND TRIAL

Kahuna Nanu v Ash
Received: Lycanium Z (Nanu decided not to give him Darkium Z as Ash didn't seem like the type of person who would use that)

To complete this Grand Trial, Ash had to defeat all three of Kahuna Nanu's Pokémon with just one of his.

BATTLE 1

 V

| KROOKODILE | LYCANROC* |

BATTLE 2

 V

| SABLEYE | LYCANROC* |

BATTLE 3

 V

| PERSIAN (ALOLAN) | LYCANROC* |

Ash and Lycanroc used Rockium-Z to do Continental Crush and win the match.

PONI ISLAND

Ash wanted to compete in a Grand Trial but Poni Island didn't have an island Kahuna for him to face. Instead, Ash decided to take on the Island Guardian, Tapu Fini, but first needed to defeat Gladion, who had had the same idea. Hapu, granddaughter of the previous Kahuna, agreed to referee the match. In doing so, she learned about Ash's experiences with previous island Kahunas and realised what it would take for her to follow in her grandfather's footsteps. While visiting the Ruins of Hope, Hapu's grandfather appeared and told her that Tapu Fini had accepted her as the new island Kahuna.

PONI ISLAND GRAND TRIAL

Kahuna Hapu v Ash
Received: Steelium Z

BATTLE 1

 V

| MUDSDALE | PIKACHU* |

Ash and Pikachu use Electrium-Z and do Gigavolt Havoc to knock Mudsdale out.

ULTRA GUARDIANS

The Ultra Guardians are part of the Aether Foundation. The group was formed by Lusamine, Gladion and Lillie's mother, to research Ultra Beasts, Ultra Wormholes and Ultra Space.

The Ultra Guardians' base is located below the Pokémon School and is overseen by Lusamine's Clefable. When the Guardians accept a mission, they shout, 'Ultroger!'

ULTRA GUARDIANS' EQUIPMENT

The team are given Beast Balls and a medical kit containing Full Restores, Max Potions and some Berries with healing properties to use during their missions.

ULTRA GUARDIANS' RIDE POKÉMON

Each Guardian has a Ride Pokémon that they use for Ultra Guardian missions.

ASH · GARCHOMP
LANA · DRAGONAIR
KIAWE · CHARIZARD
LILLIE · ALTARIA
SOPHOCLES · METANG
MALLOW · FLYGON
GLADION · NOIVERN

> *Ash, Kiawe, Gladion, Lillie, Lana, Mallow and Sophocles are the Ultra Guardians –*
> *a task force in the Alola region whose goal is to catch Ultra Beasts who stray into*
> *the Pokémon world and send them back into Ultra Space.*

WHO ARE THE ULTRA BEASTS?

BUZZWOLE

BLACEPHALON

POIPOLE

XURKITREE

STAKATAKA

NECROZMA

CELESTEELA

PHEROMOSA

ASH'S POIPOLE

Poipole first met Ash when it came through an Ultra Wormhole and became fascinated by the light produced by Pikachu's attack. Poipole didn't appear in the Pokémon database, so the friends took it back to the Ultra Guardians' Base to ask Lusamine about it. She suggested Ash keep it in his team.

Poipole is very playful and loves to express itself by drawing and spinning on its stinger when its happy. After greenery and flowers returned to Poipole's world, it returned home. It drew a large picture of Ash and Pikachu in the sand to show how much it loved them.

ULTRA GUARDIAN MISSIONS

The missions and adventures of the Ultra Guardians are of epic proportions, you might even say they are out of this world ... because they are in Ultra Space! These are some of the exciting Ultra Guardians' moments.

BUZZWOLE

This was the Ultra Guardians' very first official mission! Buzzwole entered through a wormhole above the Melemele Meadow. Pikachu's Thunderbolts weren't very effective, but when it saw Kiawe, Buzzwole flexed its muscles to show off and Kiawe did the same back! The two then had a hilarious 'Muscle Flex-off'! Ash managed to capture it in the Beast Ball while it was distracted with flexing.

CELESTEELA

Sophocles found Celesteela while he was camping with his parents. It turned out that Celesteela had arrived in the Alola region 200 years earlier and had been stuck in the ground ever since, slowly absorbing enough energy to go home. The Ultra Guardians realised that when it took off, it would set the forest ablaze! They worked together to create a defensive barrier to protect the forest and Celesteela got home safely.

PHEROMOSA

When Pheromosa entered the world, it began attacking Alolan Trainers and stealing their Z-Crystals for energy. Team Rocket's Meowth fell in love with its beauty and decided to help it find more Z-Crystals, even helping it escape the Ultra Guardians a few times. Pheromosa was eventually defeated by Bewear so Ash and the other Guardians could capture it and send it back to its home world.

STAKATAKA

Stakataka first entered the world via a wormhole above the Pokémon School, but dodged every Beast Ball the students threw at it! It escaped into the Alola region, where it was mistaken for a pedestal on a building site. A statue was put on top of it, sending it into a rage! Ash managed to removed the statue, and Stakataka calmed down when it realised the Trainer was trying to return it to its home world.

THE BATTLE WITH NECROZMA

One day, the class at Pokémon School realised all the adults seemed sleepy and unengaged. Even Professor Kukui couldn't find the energy to teach! Instead, Lillie told the class about the legend of the Blinding One.

'When the Blinding One appeared in our land, the world overflowed with a blinding, glistening light. That light had a strange and wonderful power, which created the Islands of Alola. When the Blinding One had shed all of its light, it transformed into darkness and went into a long, deep sleep. At that point, the sun and moon became flesh and appeared, sharing their own light. As it reawakened from its slumber, The Blinding One's light once again shined brightly and it spread to the ends of the sky.'

Meanwhile, the adults in town continued to act strangely. Ash and Kiawe also couldn't get their Pokémon to perform properly in battle. Something was happening to the energy in the Alola region. A small wormhole had opened up and was absorbing the region's Ultra Aura power.

Suddenly, Solgaleo and Lunala appeared, followed by a terrifying black Ultra Beast. A huge battle took place in the sky, until the beast absorbed Solgaleo and escaped through a wormhole. Lunala collapsed on to the beach. The Ultra Guardians jumped into action. The team discovered that the energy from their Z-Rings could help Lunala, so they knew they had to get to Solgaleo too. When they journeyed through the Ultra Wormhole, the Ultra Guardians found themselves in the dying world of the Poipole. A Nagandel told the Guardians through telepathy that their world flourished under the light of the Blinding One, or what they called Necrozma. But when it lost its light, their world died.

The Ultra Guardians realised they could use their Z-Power to restore Necrozma's light, but it just wasn't enough to free Solgaleo. Suddenly, in the Alola region, Tapu Koko and the other Island Guardians all started sending their energy through the wormhole. So did all the humans and Pokémon, as well as all the Poipole.

It was only when everyone worked together and shared their energy that both the Poipole world and the Alola region were able to be saved! Greenery and flowers returned, and Ash's Poipole decided to stay in its home world.

TRAINER TALES

The Alola region is a group of islands, the people who live there value friendship, having fun and protecting their Pokémon and their habitats. Ash learned a lot during his Alolan adventures.

1 MEETING TAPU KOKO

Melemele Island's Guardian, Tapu Koko, was curious about Ash and lured him into the forest. Ash couldn't find the mysterious Pokémon, but later that night, Tapu Koko returned and gave Ash a gift – a Z-Ring and Electrium-Z! Tapu Koko was rarely seen by humans but was known to give gifts to people it liked. The next day, Tapu Koko stole Ash's hat and led him back into the forest where the two agreed to battle. Tapu Koko tapped Ash's Z-Ring to activate it – he wanted Ash to use his first Z-Move! Ash and Pikachu did Gigavolt Havoc, which caused a huge explosion, shattered Ash's Z-Crystal and made Tapu Koko fly away. It was too early for Ash to use Z-Moves but he resolved to prove his worthiness.

2 NEBBY THE FRIENDLY ULTRA BEAST

One night, Ash had a strange dream that Solgaleo and Lunala had created a new Pokémon and Tapu Koko led the new Pokémon to where Ash was sleeping. This wasn't a dream though, as Ash found the Pokémon the next day in the woods. Lillie nicknamed it Nebby. When they showed Nebby to Lusamine, she recognised it as an Ultra Beast and wanted to return it to Ultra Space, but Ash refused. He knew that Solgaleo and Lunala had entrusted him with Nebby for a good reason.

3 THE FIRST TRIP TO ULTRA SPACE!

When Lusamine was taken into Ultra Space by an Ultra Beast called Nihilego, the Ultra Guardians joined Lillie and Gladion on a rescue mission. After the Island Guardians performed a ritual to open the wormhole, Ash's Nebby evolved into the mighty Solgaleo, the Legendary Sun Pokémon of the Alola region! Solgaleo invited all the friends to climb on to its back, and with the help of a new Z-Move, Ash opened an Ultra Wormhole. When they found Lusamine, Nihilego was trying to drain her energy. It was also controlling all of her Pokémon, so some epic battles ensued! Soon the team realised that fighting Lusamine's Pokémon was useless, as even after being knocked out by Z-Moves, her Pokémon quickly healed from the energy in Ultra Space. Lillie pleaded with her mum to come back to them to no avail. Finally, Ash used Pikashunium-Z so Pikachu could perform a Z-Move. Ultra Space filled with rainbow-coloured flashes of lightning, which freed Lusamine.

4 ROCKRUFF'S EVOLUTION INTO LYCANROC

After winning the final battle at Kahuna Olivia's Grand Trial, Rockruff was more aggressive than usual, which meant that it was about to evolve. Rockruff turned and bit Rowlet during the battle and, feeling upset by its actions, ran away to think and train alone. It came across Tapu Lele, who challenged it to a battle – but Rockruff was no match for the Island Guardian and was defeated. The next day, the injured Rockruff was found by Olivia and Gladion's Lycanroc, who took it to the Ruins of Life. There, Tapu Lele performed Draining Kiss and used the energy to heal Rockruff. As the setting sun turned a brilliant green, Rockruff howled and evolved into Dusk Form Lycanroc, before returning to Ash.

MANALO CONFERENCE

The **Manalo Conference** was brand new to the Alola League when Ash first entered. The winner gets to battle the famous Masked Royal in an exhibition battle.

PRELIMINARIES
These battles are refereed by the four island Kahunas – Hala, Olivia, Nanu and Hapu. All 151 Trainers put one of their Pokémon on the field, and they all fight in a giant Battle Royale until there are only 16 Trainers left!

ASH · PIKACHU
KIAWE · TURTONATOR
SOPHOCLES · TOGEDEMARU
LANA · EEVEE
MALLOW · SHAYMIN
LILLIE · SNOWY (ALOLAN VULPIX)

Jessina (Team Rocket's Jessie), Jameseo (Team Rocket's James), Gladio, Hau, Faba, Ilima, Acerola, Mina, Guzma and Samson Oak make it through to the next round.

FIRST ROUND
Astrid v Ash

Referee: Hala. The first round consists of 1-on-1 single battles. Each of the island Kahuna referees two consecutive bouts.

BATTLE · HYPNO V MELTAN*

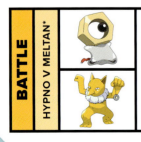

Meltan ate half of Hypno's medallion, upsetting it and knocking it out with Flash Cannon.

QUARTER-FINALS
Hau v Ash

Referee: Nanu. The eight Trainers are matched-up by a computer. Each battle is refereed by one of the island Kahunas.

BATTLE · DECIDUEYE V ROWLET*

Both Trainers opened the battle with Z-Moves. Rowlet won by landing a Brave Bird from above.

SEMI-FINALS Guzma v Ash

Referee: *Nanu. The round consists of 2-on-2 single battles. The referee of the match is selected randomly.*

BATTLE 1 SCIZOR V TORRACAT**

BATTLE 2 GOLISOPOD V TORRACAT**

BATTLE 3 SCIZOR V TORRACAT*

BATTLE 4 GOLISOPOD* V TORRACAT

BATTLE 5 GOLISOPOD V PIKACHU*

Ash charged up his Z-Ring and Pikachu launched Gigavolt Havoc, but Golisopod withstood the Z-Move! Golisopod shredded Pikachu's Electroweb with its sharp claws and countered with Poison Jab. Pikachu dodged it and finally knocked Golisopod out.

FINALS Ash v Gladion

Referee: *Professor Kukui. The finals consist of a 3-on-3 single battle to find the winner of the Manalo Conference.*

BATTLE 1 SILVALLY* V MELMETAL

BATTLE 2 SILVALLY V PIKACHU*

BATTLE 3 LYCANROC/ZOROARK**** V PIKACHU****

BATTLE 4 LYCANROC (MIDNIGHT) V LYCANROC (DUSK)*

Both Lycanroc took heavy blows from the other, but neither gave up. Gladion's Lycanroc did Stone Edge but Ash's Pokémon used Accelerock and then Counter, which knocked Gladion's Lycanroc into the wall of the stadium. Ash became Champion of the league!

EXHIBITION MATCH

Masked Royal v Ash

Referee: Hala. This exhibition battle is a full 6-on-6 battle. The battle opened with the huge reveal that the Masked Royal is actually … Professor Kukui!

BATTLE 1
TORRACAT V INCINEROAR**

Kukui had Incineroar do Blast Burn, but Torracat absorbed the energy of the move into its bell. Soon Torracat's bell started to smoke, so Ash recalled the Pokémon to rest.

BATTLE 2
LYCANROC** V INCINEROAR

In the beginning of the battle, Incineroar was still recharging from its previous Blast Burn. This allowed Lycanroc to land some direct hits, and Kukui recalled Incineroar.

BATTLE 3
LYCANROC V BRAVIARY*

Braviary flew Lycanroc high into the air and slammed it back down, but Lycanroc was still able to get back up. It was unable to dodge Superpower though, and it was defeated.

BATTLE 4
ROWLET* V BRAVIARY

Rowlet started out nervous, but Ash got it to focus. It dodged Superpower at the last second and landed Brave Bird, sending Braviary plummeting down to the ground.

BATTLE 5
ROWLET V VENUSAUR*

When Rowlet opened with Brave Bird, Venusaur responded by trapping it in its flower. Rowlet escaped but was knocked out with Sludge Bomb and Vine Whip.

BATTLE 6
TORRACAT* V VENUSAUR

With Torracat's bell still full of energy from its previous battle, its Fire Blast was unstoppable against Venusaur's Sludge Bomb and Vine Whip. Torracat took the victory.

BATTLE 7
PIKACHU V EMPOLEON**

After several huge clashes between Metal Claw and Iron Tail, Empoleon used Whirlpool to make Pikachu very dizzy. Ash had no choice but to recall his pal to recover.

BATTLE 8
MELMETAL* V EMPOLEON

Melmetal spun rapidly to avoid Empoleon's attack. It was too heavy to be affected by Empoleon's Whirlpool anyway. Melmetal won with Double Iron Bash.

BATTLE 9
MELMETAL V INCINEROAR*

Melmetal rushed in to face Incineroar, and Kukui took advantage of the close-range combat. Incineroar used Blast Burn, which engulfed Melmetal in flames and ended the battle.

BATTLE 10
NAGANADEL* V LUCARIO

Lucario held back Naganadel's main stinger to stop it doing X-Scissor. But it used its remaining stingers to do a close-range Dragon Pulse and Lucario fell in defeat.

BATTLE 11
TORRACAT* V INCINEROAR

The two Fire-type opponents performed a Z-Move at the same time, causing a huge explosion. Throat Chop and Revenge collided and Incineroar collapsed.

BATTLE 12
NAGANADEL V TAPU KOKO*

Tapu Koko was here to fight Ash! The match between an Ultra Beast and an Island Guardian was a spectacle for the ages! Tapu Koko used Dazzling Gleam to win the battle.

BATTLE 13
PIKACHU* V TAPU KOKO

After containing Tapu Koko's Nature's Madness with Electroweb, Pikachu landed a clean hit and sent Tapu Koko to the ground. All four Island Guardians gathered together and sung, giving Tapu Koko extra power for a second Legendary Z-Move. A huge, glowing giant climbed out of the ground. At that moment, Ash used Pikashunium-Z for Pikachu's 10,000,000 Volt Thunderbolt. A massive explosion engulfed the stadium, which cleared to reveal that Tapu Koko was unable to continue.

WELCOME TO THE ...
GALAR REGION

The Galar region is large, close to the Kalos region, filled with idyllic countryside, cities and snow-covered mountains. The Galar region has a long mainland area, as well as the Isle of Armour to the east. The northern, snow-covered area is called the Crown Tundra, populated by many Pokémon and separated from the rest of the region by a tall mountain range extending from coast to coast.

There are 12 cities and towns in the Galar region, with the two main cities, Hammerlocke and Motostoke, located on the Slumbering Weald plains to the north of the mountains. The skies in the region are often grey and cloudy, and the weather always changes very quickly! The Galar region is famous for holding the World Coronation Series. Trainers from all over the world come here to compete with hopes of being named the strongest Trainer in the Pokémon world!

WORLD CORONATION SERIES

The Galar region plays host to the tournament that determines the strongest Trainer. Ash is ready to face the current champion in his quest to become a Pokémon Master.

Trainers are divided into four classes and their ranking is based on their battle history and statistics.

GENERAL RULES

- Battles are judged by the Drone Rotom.
- If two opponents draw after a battle, there is no change in either Trainer's ranking.
- Trainers can only battle against others in the same class. The exception is that the top-ranked Trainers of Ultra Class can only advance if they beat the lowest-ranked Master Class member in a special entrance battle.
- Both challengers have to send out their first Pokémon at the same time.
- Challengers can switch their Pokémon out at any time.

NORMAL CLASS
- All first-time competitors are put into this class first, regardless of their previous status.
- The challengers must seek out battles with other Trainers in nearby areas, and both must agree to battle.

GREAT CLASS
- A Trainer must finish between 999th and 100th place to advance from Normal Class.
- The battle rules are the same as for Normal Class.

ULTRA CLASS
- A Trainer must finish between 99th and 9th place to advance from Great Class.
- Ultra Class battles are scheduled and the participant's opponent is decided for them. Battles in Ultra Class are usually broadcast worldwide, held in stadiums and have commentators as well as the evaluation of the Drone Rotom.
- Each challenger can use only one of the following techniques per match: Mega Evolution, Z-Moves or Dynamax.

MASTER CLASS
- This class contains the top eight Trainers in the world rankings. These are called the Masters Eight and they are certified by the Pokémon Battle Commission.
- The Trainers can change the rules of combat, as long as the competitors agree and they are accepted by the Commission before the battle.
- All Masters Eight battle each other at the end of the season in the Masters Eight Tournament, held at the Wyndon Stadium.
- At any other time in the season, any member of the Masters Eight may request a battle against any of the other seven members.
- The battle rules are the same as for Ultra Class.

ASH'S CATCHES

The Galar region brings Ash face to face with some old favourites, helping him complete some sets from his many years of adventure!

DRAGONITE

TYPE:
Dragon / Flying

Dragonite is Ash's first fully evolved Pseudo Legendary Pokémon and the only one on Ash's team. Dragonite is extremely powerful but likes nothing more than a hug! In battle, it is fierce, but turns friendly as soon as its done.

GENGAR

TYPE:
Ghost / Poison

When Ash caught Gengar, he finally had one of each Pokémon type. Gengar is very mischievous and often pranks Ash. It taunts its opponents in battle by getting close to them and sticking its tongue out.

LUCARIO

TYPE:
Fighting / Steel

Lucario is Ash's only Pokémon that can Mega Evolve. Lucario formed its link with Ash before it even hatched. After winning the World Coronation Series, it defeated Bea's Machamp in its Gigantamax form.

SIRFETCH'D

TYPE:
Fighting

A Galarian Farfetch'd is the first Pokémon that Ash caught in the Galar region. The evolved Sirfetch'd is a very proud Pokémon and always wants to learn new skills. Even when it's about to lose, it refuses to give up.

DRACOVISH

TYPE:
Water / Dragon

Dracovish is a Pokémon that was revived from a mix of different Galarian fossils. Even though it is a slow swimmer, its powerful legs mean that when it sinks to the bottom underwater, it is able to run quickly.

MR. MIME (MIMEY)

TYPE:
Psychic / Fairy

Mimey was first adopted by Ash's mum, Delia, helping her around her house and garden. When Ash moved into Cerise Lab, Delia asked Mimey to look after Ash. It helped to train Ash's Lucario when it was a newborn Riolu.

DYNAMAX AND GIGANTAMAX

Dynamax and Gigantamax are temporary transformations of a Pokémon, which drastically increase its size. Trainers who have a Dynamax Band are able to Dynamax their Pokémon, but Gigantamax can only be achieved by certain Pokémon.

Dynamax can only be used once in a battle, and only for three turns. Gigantamax is a type of Dynamax, but this power originates from the Pokémon, Eternatus. It was defeated by Zacian and Zamazenta thousands of years ago, creating power spots all across the Galar region where the Gigantamax Evolution can be triggered.

During the final of the World Coronation Series, opponents Lance and Leon used Dynamax Gyarados and Gigantamax Charizard in battle! The transformation not only made these Pokémon enormous, but it also unlocked special and more powerful Max Moves. Charizard used G-Max Wildfire and it won this titanic match-up.

The first time Ash's Pikachu transformed into Gigantamax Pikachu was to battle the Gigantamax Drednaw outside of Wyndon Stadium. Leon oversaw the battle and was shocked to see that Ash and Pikachu had managed this transformation without the Dynamax Band. He called down to tell Ash to get Pikachu to do G-Max Volt Crash, which it did to knock the Drednaw back to its regular form.

Leon told Ash that the Trainer has to recall their Pokémon into its Poké Ball to activate Dynamax. However, Pikachu doesn't go into its Poké Ball, so they would have to come up with another way. It turned out that the pair could activate the Gigantamax form through their bond alone. Pikachu took a while to master Gigantamax, losing some of its agility due to its massive size.

PROFESSOR MAGNOLIA

Professor Magnolia is the professor for the Galar region. She does research and specialises in Dynamax transformations. Her granddaughter is called Sonia.

Professor Magnolia's lab is in Wedgehurst. Professor Magnolia is very wise and noble. When Goh met her, she explained Dynamax was a special power that only existed in the Galar region.

Galar particles allowed the Pokémon there to transform at power spots. The same particles were found in Wishing Stars, a type of meteor.

Professor Magnolia wanted to use a Wishing Star in her research to find a way to control the Dynamax Phenomenon. She worked with Macro Cosmos to develop the Dynamax Bands used by Pokémon Trainers in battle. While working with Chairman Rose, they discovered that Galar particles could also be used as an energy source, but she left their partnership after becoming concerned that he did not have good intentions.

GOH

Goh grew up in Vermillion City, in the Kanto region, with his parents and his grandmother. His only friend growing up was Chloe.

When they were six years old, Chloe invited Goh to go to Professor Oak's Summer Camp with her. The pair ended up chasing a mysterious Pokémon into the woods – it was Mew. From that moment, Goh was determined that one day he would capture Mew. This encounter later developed into his passion for catching every Pokémon in the Pokédex, including each Pokémon along the family tree and any regional variants he came across.

Even though he didn't attend school very often – much to Chloe's annoyance – Goh did a lot of his own research and so is very knowledgeable about all things Pokémon. Despite all his book knowledge, he is still a rookie Trainer. As he spent so much time alone and researching, Goh is quite shy and not very good at making friends … until he meets Ash!

HOW GOH MET ASH

One day, Goh spotted a Lugia flying across the sky in Vermillion City. As he chased it down, he ran into another Trainer who was doing exactly the same thing … and that Trainer was Ash! The Lugia let the boys ride on its back, soaring over the region and into the ocean. They had such a good time, they became instant friends. When the pair reported their finding to Professor Cerise, he took them both on as research fellows in his lab. Their job was to travel all over the Pokémon world to find and meet all different kinds of Pokémon.

Goh had always dreamed that the first Pokémon he would catch would be Mew, so he turned down a first partner Pokémon from Cerise. But when he arrived in the Galar region, he teamed up with a wild Scorbunny to help a Gigantamaxed Snorlax. The pair bonded and Goh decided to catch Scorbunny as his first-ever Pokémon.

CHAIRMAN ROSE

Chairman Rose is the chairman of the Galar League, as well as being in charge of all the energy and power resources for the region.

Rose sponsored Leon during his rise through the World Coronation ranks, and he offered the same support to Ash. Ash turned him down, as he wanted to do it independently so he could uncover the true meaning of becoming a Pokémon Master.

Rose worked for many years with Professor Magnolia, researching the Galar particles to discover the source of their power. Together, they created the Dynamax Band, which is used in the Galar League.

Rose saw different uses for the research and the power of Galar particles, which led to Professor Magnolia ending their partnership.

After some digging, Leon and Ash discovered that Rose was forcing Galar particles into the core of the Power Plant, which was causing the outbreaks of Gigantamax Pokémon in the wild. These Pokémon were all over the Galar region, wreaking havoc and destroying everything around them. Rose knew all of this, but was using the particles to resurrect Eternatus, the Legendary Pokémon. Eternatus is the reason that the Galar region has the particles that cause Dynamax Evolution in the first place. Rose wanted Leon to capture Eternatus to use it as an infinite source of energy, but Leon soon realised that the Pokémon was too powerful to contain.

Ash battled Rose using Riolu, who evolved into Lucario. The chairman was defeated and fled in his helicopter. As Zacian and Zamazenta arrived to contain Eternatus, its Eternabeam smashed into Rose's helicopter and the Pokémon flew away – its whereabouts are now unknown.

WHAT'S TEAM ROCKET UP TO?

Giovanni ordered Jessie, James, Meowth and Wobbuffet to steal strong and rare Pokémon for Team Rocket, so they could be feared all over the Pokémon world.

The boss gave the trio a new bit of tech, the Rocket Prize Master. This was a Pokémon vending machine filled with Poké Balls and it was delivered to wherever the trio were by a Pelipper, carrying the tech in its beak. Meowth had to use his golden head charm to open it and it dispensed

two Poké Balls for Jessie and James to temporarily use, as well as a leaflet containing name, type and moves of the Pokémon.

JESSIE'S POKÉMON

WOOBAT

YANMEGA

GOURGEIST

WOBBUFFET | **FRILLISH**

SEVIPER

JAMES'S POKÉMON

MIME JR.

CARNIVINE

INKAY

YAMASK

MORPEKO

AMOONGUSS

ALTERNATE WORLD TEAM ROCKET

In another dimension, there was an alternative version of Team Rocket, who were a lot more successful than the trio! They successfully captured the Red Chain, which they used to make Dialga and Palkia battle each other. This battle caused all Pokémon in the alternative universe to revert back to being eggs!

Alternate Team Rocket stole all the Pokémon eggs and planned to raise them into a big Team Rocket army and take over the world.

With the balance of the Pokémon dimensions at stake, Ash, his friends and their alternate selves joined together to break the Red Chain … but all their Pokémon reverted to eggs. With no Pokémon, there was no way to win, so Ash suggested they wish for Arceus, Dialga and Palkia's creator, to return things to normal. Suddenly, Arceus appeared and immediately undid the results of the battle and sent everyone back to their dimensions.

GIGANTAMAX PIKACHU

When Leon was crowned Monarch of the World Coronation Series in Wyndon Stadium, Ash was desperate to battle him! Leon saw Gigantamax Pikachu defeat the rampaging Dynamax Drednaw outside the stadium, so agreed to the match-up. Leon gave Ash a Dynamax Band and told him this was the only way to control the Dynamax Evolution. During the battle, Ash's Dynamax Band glowed and the energy turned Pikachu into Gigantamax Pikachu again. Pikachu became big and clumsy, and its Iron Tail move became wobbly. Dynamax Charizard easily out-manoeuvred Pikachu's G-Max moves to win the battle. Ash realised that he needed to train with Pikachu while in Gigantamax form.

DEMOTION COMMOTION!

Ash's Aura connection with Riolu started when Riolu was still in its egg, but he still needed to perfect his Aura abilities. Ash and Riolu trained hard together, working on their bond and strategies. During the World Coronation Series, while in Great Class, Ash lost three times in a row. He had insisted on using Riolu but he pushed it too hard. After Riolu lost to Bea's Octillery, Ash adjusted Riolu's battle strategy from being close combat to staying a distance away from the opponent. This was a battle style they had not trained in, which resulted in Riolu losing again. Ash was demoted back to Normal Class, which knocked his confidence. His friends had to remind him that with hard work he could get back into Great Class … and all the way to the top! It's a lesson Ash has learned time and again, that no matter how badly you fail, your friends and Pokémon will always be there to lift you up!

On his journeys over the world, and in the Galar region, Ash learned many new lessons to help him become the best Trainer he could be, as he climbed the ranks in the World Coronation Series.

BE PATIENT AND PERSEVERE

Ash and Lucario battled a Mega Alakazam to get the Key Stone, allowing them to perform a Mega Evolution. Ash's third battle against Bea, after they had lost the first two, was his opportunity to prove to everyone how far he and Lucario had come. In the middle of the match, Ash tried to Mega Evolve Lucario, but Lucario turned around and refused. The announcer questioned if Ash and Lucario's bond was strong enough for a Mega Evolution, but Leon responded that it was because of Ash and Lucario's strong bond that Lucario could refuse in the first place. Ash apologised to Lucario for panicking and pushing it into Mega Evolution when it wasn't ready. Later in the match, against Gigantamax Machamp, Lucario felt it was ready and let Ash know it was the time to Mega Evolve. Listening and respecting the wishes of his Pokémon is one of Ash's biggest strengths and led him to many battle victories, including this one.

RELY ON YOUR SPECIAL SKILLS

One night, while camping in the Kalos region, Ash and Lucario sensed something through the Aura. Ash was certain it was his Greninja, who had been travelling all over the region, protecting its people and Pokémon from the destructive roots of a mysterious rock. Ash invited it to battle Lucario, but when Greninja began to win, the frustrated Lucario ran into the forest. Greninja followed it to a stream, where the pair started making ripples. Ash knew the two Pokémon were so alike, and had the same drive to be the strongest they could be. When a root erupted near Ash, it interrupted Lucario and Greninja, who both sensed that their Trainer was in danger. They attacked the roots with Greninja using Water Shuriken, and a Mega-Evolved Lucario charging up an Aura Sphere. It was in perfect sync with Ash, the sphere was the biggest one it'd ever made, and the combined attacks destroyed the roots.

TRAINER TALES

Ash makes many new friends in the Galar region and discovers lots of interesting new Pokémon too. These are some of Ash's cool moments.

1 FOSSIL MIX-UP

Ash, Goh and Chloe travelled to the Galar region to search for rare Pokémon fossils in the Wild Area. They worked with fossil researchers, Cara Liss and Bray Zenn. They tried to restore two fossils back to life, but they accidentally mixed up the fossil skeletons to create two very odd Pokémon: Dracovish and Arctozolt! After Dracovish became fond of Ash, the researchers asked Ash and Goh if they would take the Pokémon and use them in their team. They agreed!

2 THIEF ON THE LOOSE!

On their first visit to the Galar region, Ash and Goh stopped for some of the region's famous scones. The two friends became distracted by a Scorbunny, a Pokémon they had never seen before. Unbeknown to them, a group of cheeky Nickit were using the opportunity to rifle through their things looking for food! The Nickit stole Ash's backpack and a chase ensued. It turned out Scorbunny was the brains of the operation. Ash had Pikachu battle the mischievous Fire type, winning with an Electroweb.

3 THE DARKEST DAY

Sonia, Professor Magnolia's assistant, told Ash and Goh the legend of the Darkest Day:

'A long time ago, a great black storm covered the region and giant Pokémon ran rampant, but the chaos was eventually stopped by a single young hero wielding a sword and a shield.'

Chairman Rose was experimenting with Galar particles at the Power Plant in the hope of using the energy to fuel the Galar region. His work resulted in another Darkest Day! Eternatus, the Legendary Pokémon, had broken free from the core. Goh and Sonia realised that the legend was wrong; it wasn't just one hero that saved the day, but two. One would hold the sword and the other the shield. Ash headed to Hammerlocke Stadium to battle Eternatus and Chairman Rose. Ash sent in Pikachu and Riolu against Rose's Ferrothorn and Copperajah. Rose's Pokémon cornered Pikachu and Riolu, but Ash had them jump to avoid Power Whip, causing Ferrothorn and Copperajah to hit each other instead. Riolu evolved into Lucario mid-battle and used its new move, Aura Sphere, to defeat Ferrothorn and Copperajah. Ash then went to help Leon battle Eternatus, which soon evolved into its Eternamax form. It unleashed an Eternabeam into the stadium.

At this crucial moment, Goh arrived with the legendary sword and shield, which began to glow. Ash and Goh realised that they must fulfil the legend. Zamazenta and Zacian suddenly appeared, taking their Crowned Sword and Crowned Shield forms, ready to battle Eternatus. Ash, Goh and Leon combined their attacks with the two Legendary Pokémon, in order to weaken Eternatus. Finally Goh, with Ash's help, threw a Poké Ball and caught Eternatus, ending the Darkest Day.

WORLD CORONATION SERIES

NORMAL

GREAT

ASH
(RANK TBD)
V
VISQUEZ
(RANK 2109)

BATTLE 1
Pikachu v
Raichu**

BATTLE 2
Gengar* v
Raichu

BATTLE 3
Gengar v
Electrode*

BATTLE 4
Pikachu* v
Electrode

ASH
(3763)
V
OLIVER
(UNKNOWN)

BATTLE 1
Pikachu* v
Meganium

ASH
(1512)
V
LOB
(UNKNOWN)

BATTLE 1
Pikachu* v
Clawitzer

ASH
(1022)
V
KORRINA
(1001)

BATTLE 1
Gengar** v
Mienshao

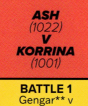

BATTLE 2
Gengar v
Lucario*

BATTLE 3
Dragonite* v
Mienshao

BATTLE 4
Dragonite* v
Lucario

ASH
(921)
V
TONY
(UNKNOWN)

BATTLE 1
Riolu* v
Electabuzz

ASH
(901)
V
KRICKETINA
KYLIE *(895)*

BATTLE 1
Pikachu* v
Kricketune

Ash entered the World Coronation Series, a tournament to decide the strongest Trainer in the Pokémon world! He needed to fight lots of experienced Trainers to work his way up the rankings, so he could face Leon, the current champion.

* winner
** winner after a match withdrawal
*** forced withdrawal into Poké Ball
**** double KO
***** faints

NORMAL

GREAT

ASH
(890)
V
BEA
(751)

BATTLE 1
Farfetch'd v Hawlucha*

BATTLE 2
Riolu v Grapploct*

ASH
(930)
V
TRAINER
(UNKNOWN)

BATTLE 1
Riolu v Octillery*

ASH
(975)
V
TRAINER
(UNKNOWN)

BATTLE 1
Riolu v Tentacruel*

With this loss, Ash was demoted back to Normal Class.

ASH
(1021)*
V
BEA
(193)

BATTLE 1
Pikachu* v Hitmontop

BATTLE 2
Pikachu v Grapploct*

BATTLE 3
Riolu** v Grapploct**

Ash battled to get his rank back up to 451, so he returned to Great Class.

ASH
(451)
V
DOZER
(UNKNOWN)

BATTLE 1
Farfetch'd* v Gurdurr

Ash's rank rises from 381 to 273.

ASH
(273)
V
RINTO
(UNKNOWN)

BATTLE 1
Farfetch'd \ Sirfetch'd* v Gallade

Farfetch'd evolved into Sirfetch'd mid-battle!

ASH
(184)
V
IRIS
(UNKNOWN)

BATTLE 1
Dragonite v Dragonite**

BATTLE 2
Dracovish* v Dragonite

BATTLE 3
Dracovish v Haxorus*

BATTLE 4
Dragonite* v Haxorus

WORLD CORONATION SERIES

ULTRA

ASH (99) V VOLKNER (27)

BATTLE 1
Lucario v
Luxray**

BATTLE 2
Gengar** v
Luxray

BATTLE 3
Gengar v
Fan Rotom*

BATTLE 4
Pikachu** v
Fan Rotom

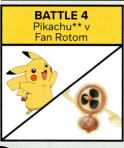

BATTLE 5
Pikachu v
Electivire**

BATTLE 6
Lucario** v
Electivire

BATTLE 7
Lucario**** v
Fan Rotom****

BATTLE 8
Pikachu* v
Electivire

ASH (64) V BEA (UNKNOWN)

BATTLE 1
Pikachu v
Grapploct**

BATTLE 2
Lucario** v
Grapploct

BATTLE 3
Lucario** v
Hawlucha

BATTLE 4
Lucario v
Machamp**

BATTLE 5
Sirfetch'd ** v Machamp

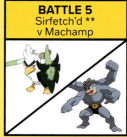

ASH (36) V MARNIE (29)

BATTLE 1
Gengar* v
Grimmsnarl

ASH (15) V DRASNA (12)

BATTLE 1
Sirfetch'd v Noivern**

BATTLE 2
Dracovish** v Noivern

BATTLE 3
Dracovish v Altaria**

BATTLE 4
Sirfetch'd**** v Altaria****

BATTLE 5
Dracovish* v Noivern

ASH (9) V RAIHAN (7)

BATTLE 1
Dragonite v Flygon**

BATTLE 2
Gengar* v Flygon

BATTLE 3
Gengar**** v Goodra****

BATTLE 4
Lucario* v Duraludon

With this win, Ash reached number eight in the rankings and entered Master Class!

203

RETURN TO THE ...
KANTO REGION

After winning the Manalo Conference, Ash decided to return home to the Kanto region. While he was there, he enjoyed all the comforts of home, saw his mum and stopped by Oak Laboratory to visit Professor Oak. Ash's old mentor mentioned that a new lab was opening in Vermillion City and he invited Ash to attend the opening ceremony.

When Ash and his new friend Goh arrived, Professor Cerise was so impressed with them that he asked them to become research fellows at his lab. In their new roles, Ash and Goh would use Cerise Lab as their home base and travel all over the Pokémon world to research Pokémon in their natural habitats.

CHLOE

Chloe grew up in Vermilion City, in the Kanto region, with her parents, Professor Cerise and Talia, as well as her brother, Parker.

Chloe and Goh have been close friends for their whole lives. In fact, before he met Ash, Chloe was Goh's only friend. People think Chloe is quiet, but she is just very cautious and realistic. She is not sure about what her hopes and dreams are, and what she should be doing in the future.

Chloe's family were given Yamper as a gift, and it instantly took a liking to Chloe. She didn't like it at first, but after it protected Chloe from Gengar, they grew to love each other. Her first partner Pokémon was Eevee, which she and Yamper rescued from Team Rocket. This was the first time Chloe really wanted to capture and train a Pokémon.

While Chloe was travelling through the Sinnoh region with Ash and Goh, she met Dawn. The two were not fast friends but after they battled a Rhydon together, they learned to respect each other. Dawn advised Chloe that trying new things was an important step in finding out what she wanted to do. When Chloe was in the Hoenn region, she was encouraged to enter the local Pokémon contest. Though Chloe and Eevee were nervous to begin with, they both performed beautifully. Chloe thought being a Pokémon performer could be the right path for her. But her travels with Ash and Goh led her to realise that she wanted to become a Pokémon researcher in the lab, like her father.

CERISE LABORATORY RESEARCH

This Pokémon Research Lab is in Vermilion City and is run by Professor Cerise. His aim is to research and document all he can learn about Pokémon, how they live and thrive in the world.

PROFESSOR CERISE

Professor Oak saw how clever Cerise was, even when he was young, and took him on as one of his protegees. He is calm, friendly and very enthusiastic about anything to do with Pokémon ... much to the embarrassment of Chloe!

ASH AND GOH

Ash and Goh use Cerise Lab as their base of operations for their adventures all over the Pokémon world. There is a domed area into Cerise Park where all the Pokémon Goh and Ash caught during their research missions can live.

REN AND CHRYSA

Cerise's lab assistants help him with his research, Chrysa is very calm, but does have a competitive side. Her favourite Pokémon is Psyduck. Ren is very knowledgeable about Pokémon, but often looks a little bit scruffy. He has a Magnemite called Francois as his partner.

PROJECT MEW

Trainers from all over the world team up to research the origins of the Mythical Pokémon, Mew. It is a project led by Professor Amaranth.

Trainers go into two categories in Project Mew: Challengers and Chasers. Challengers receive challenges and trial missions to earn tokens. Trial missions are brought to Challengers by a Corviknight. The Challengers who have earned the most tokens by the end of the Chaser Selection become Chasers.

Goh, who has wanted to catch Mew since his first sighting, is inspired to join the project when he and Ash saw Gary Oak completing one of his trial missions. Goh first had to go through a qualifier to see if he was able to take part in Chaser Selection. He had to go into the mountains of the Kanto region and capture the Alolan Ninetails who was stuck there, within six hours. Goh gained the Ninetails' trust and was able to complete his qualifier mission.

As a Challenger, Goh had to collect Volcarona's scales, catch a wild Kingdra, battle against an Articuno, join a battle royale and catch a Regieleki and Regidrago. Goh excitedly called Ash to tell him that these missions had earned him enough tokens to become a Chaser. He headed off to embark on more adventures for Project Mew.

207

TRAINER TALES

FROM ASH'S JOURNEYS

Ash's role as researcher for Cerise Lab allowed him to go all over the Pokémon world! That meant Ash could reunite with old friends. Here are some stories from his travels.

1 LAPRAS FROM THE ORANGE ISLANDS

One day, Ash, Misty and Brock were watching Wailmer bounce around on the shore, when they noticed a familiar face swimming towards them. It was Lapras, Ash's friend from the Orange Islands! It was there to ask for Ash's help. It led the friends to a cave where a Wailmer was stuck in a hole. After working together, the friends managed to free Wailmer, which was so happy that it bounced straight back into the hole and then evolved into Wailord. The problem got a whole lot bigger and heavier! Pikachu spotted Team Rocket spying on them from their submarine and had an idea. It threatened to shock the trio into blasting off – again – unless they helped them rescue the

Wailord. The trio lent a hand and, along with lots of wild Pokémon, they all worked together to pull Wailord out of the hole. At the same time Ash, Bayleef and Heracross tickled its tummy from underneath! Ash said goodbye to Lapras again, and thanked it for getting him involved in such a fun rescue!

2 A LEGENDARY CATCH!

In the Johto region, there was a legend that told of a Suicune, which appeared to clean up polluted lakes before leaving. For some reason, it was now sticking around near a particular lake. Ash and Goh were sent to investigate and discovered that the lake was being intentionally polluted. A group of Pokémon hunters were trying to lure Suicune there. They wanted it to use its powers repeatedly to clean the lake, which would weaken it and then they could capture it. The Pokémon hunters battled with Suicune and severely injured it, while also attacking Ash and Goh to stop them from being able to help. In a moment of desperation, Goh threw a Poké Ball at Suicune … and he managed to catch the Legendary Aura Pokémon! Goh helped Suicune heal its wounds, gave it some berries and the pair became friends. When Suicune was healed, Goh tried to release it so that it could continue with its important work, but instead it willingly returned to the ball to show that it wished to stay with Goh. Later, Suicune left Cerise Lab, choosing to roam alone. Goh would miss it, but knew that Suicune was always with him, even if he couldn't see it.

3 MIMEY'S FIRST (AND ONLY!) BATTLE

Ash and Goh travelled to the Hoenn region to compete in the Battle Frontier's Flute Cup. They met Hodge, who was confident that he would win the competition – and it seemed that he might be right! He quickly defeated Goh's Scyther and Scorbunny with just Mightyena, and knocked Goh out of the competition. In the final, it was Ash versus Hodge. Ash's Mimey dodged Hariyama's Force Palm and used Reflect to stop all direct hits, before finally knocking it out using Psychic. Ash then went on to win the match and the Flute Cup. This battle was Mimey's first time on Ash's team, as well as its first-ever battle, and it was a victory! Mimey won admiration from everyone, including the match commentator, but it wasn't what it wanted. It quickly let Ash know that it had lost its will to battle and it never entered a match again!

4 PIPLUP VERSUS CROAGUNK

Ash and Goh were checking out some Tentacool off the coast of Vermilion City, when they spotted an exhausted Piplup swimming in the sea. 'This Piplup is quite far from home,' remarked Ash. When they took Piplup back to Cerise Lab, they learned that its Trainer, Lauren, had been searching for it, so Ash and Goh decided to travel to the Sinnoh region to reunite them. It turned out that Piplup was in a fierce rivalry with Lauren's other Pokémon, Croagunk. Piplup challenged Croagunk to a Pokémon Iceberg Race – the winner would prove they were the best swimmer. But suddenly Team Rocket arrived to cause chaos! When Lauren was put in danger, Piplup and Croagunk put their differences aside and worked together to save their Trainer!

5 FRIENDS ACHIEVING THEIR DREAMS!

A return to the Unova region meant a reunion with Ash's friend, Iris! She was now Unova League Champion and her Axew had evolved into Haxorus. Iris was closer than ever to becoming a Dragon Master, which was always her dream. Ash was thrilled to face her in battle, sending in his Dragonite to face hers. During the match, Iris communicated with Ash's Dragonite and when it cried out in pain, Iris stopped her attacks. She spoke to it telepathically and told it to have fun in battle, and then Ash would too. When Ash asked Iris what they'd talked about, she winked and told him it was a secret. Ash's success in the battle finally moved him into Ultra Class, and he also got to see first-hand how his friend had become an incredible Dragon Trainer.

6 WITH A LITTLE HELP FROM FRIENDS

Ash's next battle was against Drasna from the Elite Four, but first, he travelled over to the Kalos region to visit Clemont and Bonnie. During a training session, Clemont noticed that Ash's Sirfetch'd was struggling to master Meteor Assault, its signature move. As per usual, Clemont had a Clemontic device for this: the Pokémon Motion Capture 1! He performed an analysis to find out the problem. After reviewing the footage, Clemont saw that Sirfetch'd's tummy was wobbling during the build-up for the move, which meant it lost energy. Luckily Dracovish came along and nibbled on

Sirfetch'd's leek, which somehow stabilised Sirfetch'd. It was now able to master the move! It was an unusual training strategy, which came about entirely by accident, but a win is a win!

7 THE ALOLA LEAGUE CHAMPION RETURNS!

To celebrate the first Alolan League Champion's return to the Alola region, they held a Battle Royale. Four Trainers and their Pokémon entered the ring, but only one would be the winner! The contestants were Ash and Pikachu, Kukui and Incineroar, Kiawe and Marowak, and Gladion and Lillie the Nihilego. The battle opened with all three Pokémon attacking Pikachu, but Pikachu impressed everyone with its speed and dodged all the attacks at once. Eventually it was just Ash versus Kukui. Ash realised that the whole crowd was cheering 'Champion!' – they were cheering for him and Pikachu! Ash enjoyed the moment and then, after urging from Gladion and Kiawe to show them his full power, Ash tossed his hat to Pikachu. They did the Z-Move 10,000,000 Volt Thunderbolt against Incineroar's Malicious Moonsault Z-Move. After the battle, Kukui and Ash were together on the beach when Tapu Koko appeared and did a little dance to send Ash good thoughts and luck. All of the Alola region joined together to give Ash confidence and support for his journey through the Masters Eight Tournament.

8 SEARCHING FOR HO-OH

Professor Cerise sent Ash and Goh to Ecruteak City in the Johto region to investigate some rumoured sightings of the Legendary, Ho-Oh. But when they arrived, they discovered that it was actually a model of Ho-Oh created by a boy called Chad. Chad's grandfather, Jaye, had been searching for Ho-Oh for many years and actually had one of its rainbow feathers. After many years of disappointment, Jaye became convinced that Ho-Oh wasn't real, but Ash knew it was, as he had seen Ho-Oh too. Ash, Goh and Chad took Jaye up to the top of Ecruteak Tower to call out for Ho-Oh, but when nothing happened, Ash, Goh and Chad left. Jaye wanted one last look up in the sky. Suddenly, a rainbow appeared and below it flew the Legendary, Ho-Oh. Jaye's dream to see Ho-Oh once more had come true.

9 PIKACHU'S ORIGIN STORY

One day, a Pichu was attacked by an Ekans in the forests around Pallet Town. It used Thunder Shock to defend itself, but was exhausted. When it recovered, it found itself all alone, until it ran into a herd of Kangaskhan. Pichu was adopted by a Kangaskhan mother and she put it in its pouch with her baby Kangaskhan. Pichu lived with the herd for a while and was happy. Baby Kangaskhan and Pichu both grew bigger until Pichu realised how difficult it was for its adoptive mother to carry them both around. Pichu realised it was time to move on. In the middle of the night Pichu crept out of the cave, and full of love and gratitude for its Kangaskhan family evolved into Pikachu. It then ran back towards Pallet Town … and the rest is Pokémon history!

10 JEALOUS PIKACHU

When Ash was deep in the middle of training with Riolu, Pikachu started to feel jealous. Ash's mum, Delia, came to visit them at Cerise Lab, and after they had dinner, Ash headed straight back out to train with Riolu. Pikachu was very cross, but Delia talked to it and put it to sleep by singing it a lullaby. The next morning, Pikachu watched Delia leave to go back to Pallet Town, and decided to follow her back. It wanted to leave Ash, who had told it to be patient while he went to train with Riolu yet again. Mimey chased Pikachu all the way back to Pallet Town, trying to convince Pikachu to return to Ash. As soon as Ash realised Pikachu was gone, he raced home to meet Pikachu. Ash apologised and Pikachu jumped into his arms and gave him a friendly Thunder Shock to show that all was forgiven!

11 GARY OAK RETURNS!

When Ash and Goh travelled to visit Professor Oak in the Kanto region, Ash took some time to visit all his Pokémon who lived in the Oak Corral. But when he got there, he found that Infernape was missing! The two friends set off on a mission to find Infernape, and on the way, they ran into Ash's old friend, Gary Oak. He gave Goh a hard time, wanting to know if he was a good enough Trainer to be friends with Ash. Goh was offended, but Ash just laughed. Gary had given him a hard time like this all his life! The trio then continued the search for Infernape, and they found it trying to challenge the Legendary Fire Bird, Moltres. Moltres accepted the challenge. After a fierce and fiery battle, Gary claimed a fallen Moltres feather as part of his research for Project Mew.

WORLD CORONATION SERIES

ROUND 1

These are 3-on-3 battles. There are no restrictions on time or exchanges, but each Trainer can use one of either Dynamax, Z-Move or Mega Evolution per match.

MATCH 1

LEON* V ALAIN

BATTLE 1
Rillaboom* v Chesnaught

BATTLE 2
Rillaboom v Charizard*

BATTLE 3
Charizard** v Charizard

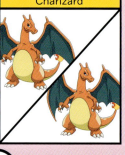

BATTLE 4
Charizard* v Malamar

BATTLE 5
Charizard* v Charizard

MATCH 2

DIANTHA* V LANCE

BATTLE 1
Aurorus v Dragonite*

BATTLE 2
Gourgeist* v Red Gyarados

BATTLE 3
Gourgeist v Hydreigon*

BATTLE 4
Gardevoir* v Hydreigon

BATTLE 5
Gardevoir* v Dragonite

After a lot of hard work climbing up the ranks, Ash finally made the Masters Eight Tournament! Ash was very excited, and after a lot of adventures and a lot of training, he was ready for whatever might be thrown his way. Ash entered the tournament ranked eight. Each member of the Masters Eight battles another member in Wyndon Stadium.

* winner
** winner after a
   match withdrawal
*** forced withdrawal
   into Poké Ball
**** double KO
***** faints

ASH'S TEAM
ASH'S TEAM
Infernape
Dragonite
Gengar
Dracovish
Pikachu
Sirfetch'd

MATCH 3

IRIS V CYNTHIA*

BATTLE 1
Excadrill* v
Gastrodon

BATTLE 2
Excadrill v
Milotic*

BATTLE 3
Dragonite v
Milotic*

BATTLE 4
Haxorus* v
Milotic

BATTLE 5
Haxorus v
Garchomp*

MATCH 4

ASH* V STEVEN STONE

BATTLE 1
Dracovish** v
Metagross

BATTLE 2
Dracovish v
Aggron*

BATTLE 3
Gengar* v
Aggron

BATTLE 4
Gengar v
Cradily*

BATTLE 5
Pikachu* v
Cradily

BATTLE 6
Pikachu* v
Metagross

ROUND 2

The winners face each other in 6-on-6 battles. There are no restrictions on time or exchanges, but each Trainer can use one of either Dynamax, Z-Move or Mega Evolution per match.

MATCH 1

LEON* V DIANTHA

Ash and his friends started watching this battle after Diantha had lost four Pokémon and Leon only one.

BATTLE 6
Rillaboom* v Goodra

BATTLE 7
Rillaboom v Gardevoir*

BATTLE 8
Charizard* v Gardevoir

MATCH 2

ASH* V CYNTHIA

BATTLE 1
Dragonite v Spiritomb*

BATTLE 2
Gengar** v Roserade

BATTLE 3
Gengar v Spiritomb*

BATTLE 4
Pikachu** v Togekiss

BATTLE 5
Pikachu* v Gastrodon

BATTLE 6
Pikachu**** v Spiritomb****

BATTLE 7
Dracovish** v Garchomp

BATTLE 8
Dracovish* v
Roserade

BATTLE 9
Dracovish v
Milotic*

BATTLE 10
Sirfetch'd* v
Milotic

BATTLE 12
Lucario* v
Togekiss

BATTLE 11
Sirfetch'd* v
Garchomp

BATTLE 13
Lucario* v
Garchomp

FINAL

The winner of this battle will be crowned Monarch! This is a 6-on-6 battle. At Leon's urging, the rules are changed so that each Trainer can use Dynamax, Z-Move and Mega Evolution all once – so the Trainer can be showcased with their full power.

ASH* V LEON

BATTLE 1
Pikachu v
Cinderace**

BATTLE 2
Gengar* v
Inteleon

BATTLE 3
Gengar v
Mr Rime*

BATTLE 4
Sirfetch'd v
Mr Rime**

BATTLE 5
Lucario* v
Mr Rime

BATTLE 6
Lucario v
Dragapult**

BATTLE 7
Dracovish*** v
Dragapult

BATTLE 8
Dragonite*** v
Dragapult

BATTLE 9
Lucario v
Dragapult*

BATTLE 10
Dragonite* v
Dragapult

BATTLE 11
Dragonite v
Rillaboom*

BATTLE 12
Sirfetch'd v
Rillaboom*

BATTLE 13
Dracovish* v
Rillaboom

BATTLE 14
Dracovish v
Cinderace*

BATTLE 15
Pikachu** v
Charizard

BATTLE 16
Pikachu* v Charizard / Cinderace

Pikachu was Ash's last Pokémon and last hope for a win. Leon recalled Cinderace so he could finish on a high with his mighty Charizard. The two long-time Trainers wanted to battle with their most loyal partners.

Leon began by Gigantamaxing Charizard, but this didn't phase Pikachu who started strong with a Thunderbolt. Charizard countered with Max Rockfall causing a sandstorm, followed by Max Wyrmwind. Pikachu was left winded,

so Ash decided it was time for a Z-Move. Leon was thrilled – he had always wanted to see Gigantamax against a Z-Move! The stadium shook with all the energy. Leon recalled a collapsed Cinderace and sent back in his ace, Charizard.

BATTLE 17
Pikachu* v Charizard

Pikachu opened the battle with Quick Attack. The opponents had a series of back-and-forth moves. Charizard used Ancient Power, and Pikachu jumped from rock to rock until it got to the arc of the stadium. As Pikachu ran back down, Charizard pursued it using Air Slash with Pikachu hitting each attack away with Iron Tail. Charizard then used Fire Blast. Pikachu tried to defend itself with Thunderbolt but it was too late. When the smoke cleared, Pikachu was still standing but breathing heavily, and then it fell over.

After remembering Ash and all of their friends were behind them, Pikachu stood up and unleashed a huge jolt of electricity. In an epic final attack, Pikachu used Thunderbolt and Charizard used Fire Blast in a head-on collision. Following the clash, both Pokémon were pushed backwards, and Charizard collapsed after a final fiery roar.

Ash was crowned Monarch of the World Coronation Series! An exhausted Pikachu jumped into his arms.

Leon presented the trophy to the new champion, Ash Ketchum!

TRAVELLING WITH OLD FRIENDS

After winning the World Coronation Series, Ash decided to travel around some more, and he ran into Misty and Brock, his friends from the very beginning of his journey. They helped him to discover how he wanted his Pokémon journey to continue and got him a little closer to answering the question, what does it mean to be a Pokémon Master?

THE ROAD MOST TRAVELLED!

Ash and Pikachu were walking through the countryside, when they arrived at a fork in the road. Ash threw up a stick in the air and declared that he would go whichever way the leaves of the stick pointed. The stick landed to the left, but Ash decided he was going to go to the right. Pikachu cheekily shocked his hat off his head in protest, but then followed Ash down the right-hand path. While wandering around, Ash spotted something mysterious crash out of the sky and into a lake. He rushed to help the severely injured Latias. Ash rescued it from the lake and nursed it back to health. It flew away, but it still kept a close eye on Ash on his travels. It was here that Ash decided that his journey would continue by him meeting Pokémon and saying goodbye.

MEETING UP WITH OLD FRIENDS!

While fishing one day, Ash ran into his friend, Misty, who was also fishing for a Clauncher. The two friends had a battle to decide who would catch the Clauncher. Misty and her Politoad defeated Ash and Corphish. The next day, while eating at a cafe, Ash and Misty felt as though they recognised the delicious food … Brock was the chef! The three friends decided to travel together again, and on their way they befriended and helped lots of Pokémon. While hiking up a mountain to see some Magikarp swimming up a waterfall, they came across a Beartic who could not control its ice powers. It had frozen everything, including the waterfall! Ash managed to calm down the scared Beartic and promised to help it train. Along with Pikachu, Talonflame and Incineroar, Ash, displaying his love of Pokémon and a willingness to go the extra mile, helped Beartic learn to control and focus its ice powers. Ash also helped to reunite a Baynet with their Trainer, a Nurse Joy, after years of being apart. As a child, Nurse Joy moved house and she accidentally left her toy behind. That toy became the Baynet. This reunion was another bond of friendship between human and Pokémon that Ash helped to strengthen.

THE SAME MOON, NOW AND FOREVER!

Later on in their travels, Pikachu was blasted off (again!) with Team Rocket. Pikachu and Meowth ended up down the river, and Pikachu instinctively knew which way to go to be reunited with Ash. At the same time, Ash had the same instinct and Brock explained that, 'Their hearts are always together, even when they're apart.' A number of incidents kept the two apart, and as night-time fell, both Ash and Pikachu found themselves looking up at the moon, thinking of each other. 'I get the feeling Pikachu is looking at the moon too,' Ash said. The next morning, the friends are joyfully reunited.

GOODBYE TO TEAM ROCKET!

The boss of Team Rocket, Giovanni, was fed up of looking after the trio's Pokémon, so he sent them back to Jessie and James. Delighted to be reunited with their beloved Pokémon, they decided to use all of them together to capture Pikachu, once and for all. They concocted a plan and managed to isolate Pikachu. When they made their attack, Latias, who had been watching over Ash for a while, used its Psychic powers to warn Ash that Pikachu was in trouble. Ash quickly arrived to battle with Team Rocket, but was quickly overwhelmed by the sheer number of Pokémon. Thankfully, the loyal Latias joined the fight and Team Rocket were blasted away … again!

LATIAS AND LATIOS

Latias used Sight Sharing with Ash to show him a vision of how it had been separated from Latios, in the hopes that Ash would help them reunite. Ash saw that Latios was being chased by a Pokémon hunter on a Hydreigon. After they found Latios healing in a cave, it turned out that they had accidentally led the Pokémon hunter straight to it. Although initially distrustful of the Trainer, Latios teamed up with Ash to save Latias and defeated the hunter with a huge Aura Sphere. Latias and Latios returned to their home as Ash decided to return himself to Pallet Town.

LET'S GO HOME!

After working so hard and for so long to be crowned Pokémon Champion of the World, Ash returned to Pallet Town. How does Ash's journey continue from here now he's achieved his dream ... or has he?

After having new adventures with Misty and Brock, it was time to say goodbye. Misty was going back to Vermillion City and Brock to Pewter City; both were going to be gym leaders again.

Ash and Pikachu were so excited to be back in Pallet Town, it was always wonderful to have all the comforts of home, in particular his mum Delia's wonderful cooking. She had bought him some brand-new shoes, as his old ones were dirty and worn out. But Ash was happy in his old shoes. He ran off to visit Professor Oak.

While Ash was at Oak Laboratory, he helped welcome the new first partner Pokémon. Charmander had gone missing so Ash helped locate it in a cave. On his way out, he ran into his old rival and friend, Gary Oak. He congratulated Ash on his victory and asked, 'Now that you're Pokémon Champion, just how close are you to being a Pokémon Master?' Ash had no answer.

WHAT IS A POKÉMON MASTER?

Ash had been dreaming of being a Pokémon Master every day of his journey, but Gary's question had left him thinking about what it really means.

Chloe had asked Ash about his dreams once.
'My dream is to be a Pokémon Master,' said Ash.
'You wanna be the top Pokémon Trainer in the world?' she asked.
'It's much more than that, way, way beyond that!' he responded.

One day, in Viridian Forest, it suddenly started to rain, so Ash and Pikachu sheltered under a tree. As they sat there, lots of other Pokémon joined them to escape the storm. As he looked at each Pokémon, Ash realised being Champion wasn't his goal.

'I want to go on a lot more adventures, and meet lots more Pokémon. And take everything I learn every day and put it to good use,' he told Pikachu. 'I want to be friends with all the Pokémon in the world. That's what it means to be a Pokémon Master.'

When the rain stopped and revealed a rainbow, Ash asked Pikachu if he'd be by his side when he really became a Pokémon Master. Pikachu joyfully agreed. It was finally time for new shoes.

After leaving home, Ash came to a fork in the path. He asked Pikachu which way he wanted to go. Pikachu fetched a stick and Ash threw it in the air … they were both ready to continue their adventures and journey together.